# MUSTANG

## RED BOOK

## Early 1965-1990

Peter C. Sessler

*Special thanks to Paul McLaughlin, Rick Kopec, Eric Binns, Wayne Houghtaling, SAAC's Shelby American World Registry and Ford Motor Company.*

First published in 1990 by Motorbooks International Publishers & Wholesalers, P O Box 2, 729 Prospect Avenue, Osceola, WI 54020 USA

Library of Congress Cataloging-in-Publication Data
Mustang red book, 1964 1/2-90 / edited by Peter C. Sessler.
　　　p.　cm. — (Motorbooks International red book series)
　　ISBN 0-87938-420-4
　　1. Mustang automobile—History.　I. Sessler, Peter C.
　II. Series.
　TL215.M8M88　1990　　　　　　　　　90-6682
　629.222'2—dc20　　　　　　　　　　　　CIP

**On the front cover:** This rare, 428CJ-powered 1968½ Fastback GT is owned by Robert Bauman.

Printed and bound in the United States of America

# Contents

# Introduction

*The Mustang Red Book* is designed to help the Mustang enthusiast determine authenticity and originality of any production Mustang built from 1965 through 1990. Each chapter covers a single model year of Mustang production and lists production figures, VIN decoding information, engine codes, exterior color codes, interior trim codes, pricing and option information and selected facts. As Mustangs keep increasing in value, the possibility of buying a fake or a "counterfeit" increases, too.

Every effort has been made to ensure the accuracy of the information presented here, which is applicable to the great majority of Mustangs built. However, there are exceptions. Because of the nature of the automobile business, Ford, like other auto manufacturers, deals with thousands of vendors and there are thousands of parts that go into the making of a Mustang. The possibility of shortages, substitutions, deletions and the like is always there, which results in a Mustang that doesn't quite fit published specifications. Most of the variations you'll find are relatively minor detail items, not something that changes the basic specifications of the car in question. For example, I doubt you'll find a six-cylinder Shelby.

The most important number in any Mustang is the VIN or Vehicle Identification Number. From 1965 to 1980, this was an eleven-digit number which broke down to model year, assembly plant, body code, engine code and consecutive unit number. Starting with 1981, Mustangs used a seventeen-digit number which, in addition to the previous information, included a vehicle manufacturer code and type of restraint system used. The VIN is stamped on various places on the car, sometimes requiring disassembly to see them.

For titling and registration purposes, there is one specific area where the manufacturer must affix the vehicle's VIN. For 1965-67 Mustangs, the number was stamped on the driver's side inner fender panel on a notch, between the shock tower and radiator support. In 1968, it was stamped on a plate which was riveted to the edge of the instrument panel on the passenger side, and was visible through the windshield. From 1969 to the present, the plate was moved over to the driver's side.

The VIN, along with additional information (see appendix), is also stamped on a metal warranty plate and riveted on the rear face of the driver's door on Mustangs built from 1965 to 1969. From 1970 to the present, Ford stopped using metal plates, substituting a vehicle certification label. The additional information consists of body type, color code, interior trim code, axle ratio code, transmission code and DSO which stands for District Special Order, which is an internal Ford code used for production.

This warranty plate and label method of identification is an area which, unfortunately, has been abused by some Mustang owners. Many Mustang vendors sell blank VIN and warranty plates and labels to Mustang owners who want a "new" plate to replace a damaged original or just to reproduce the Mustang's true original state, especially if the original door was replaced somewhere along the way. Most vendors require that the present owner verify through a copy of a title or other papers the Mustang's original VIN. The problem is that the Mustang's current owner can specify a color and interior, for example, that is not original, boosting its value. Makes you wonder how many of those early Mustangs (especially convertibles) with Pony Interiors are original. With new warranty plates, it's easy to misrepresent. You can purchase blank VIN plates, too.

Mustangs also have a "broadcast sheet," a printout showing the VIN and the options that the car was built with. It is located underneath the carpets or trunk, or sometimes taped around one of the wiring harnesses beneath the dash. An original broadcast sheet is a good way to check originality.

With the exception of 1965-66 (and some 1967) Shelby GT350s, Boss 302s and Boss 429s, you cannot match a specific engine with the Mustang in which it originally was installed. Ford did not stamp the block or heads with the car's VIN. However, with the Shelby and Boss Mustangs, knowing that the numbers match increases authenticity and value.

Ford also attached a stamped plate, usually under one of the coil hold-down bolts, which supplied engine information. Carburetors, too, got a small tag. It's easy to see that over the years, it is possible for one of these plates to be misplaced and lost during a rebuild.

There is also a riveted plate with additional information such as the consecutive unit number and option codes located under the hood. Its location varies with the plant where the car was built and with the year. Some places to look for it are behind the headlights on the radiator support on Dearborn built Mustangs and near the right side hood hinge and on the sides of the engine compartment on Metuchen built cars. San Jose Mustangs did not get a plate.

The colors and interior trim listed in each chapter are correct as far as they go. However, Ford built and will build Mustangs in colors other than those normally listed. The color section on the warranty plate or label in such cases is usually left blank.

The list of options is assembled from many different sources. The possibility always exists that some options were never installed in any Mustang or that some Mustangs may have options that were never listed in any published factory literature. Some options were deleted during the model year and some added. In the same way, prices changed throughout the model year.

Although every effort has been made to make sure that the information contained in *The Mustang Red Book* is correct, I cannot assume any responsibility for any loss arising from use of this book.

# Chapter 1

# 1965 Mustang

## Production Figures — Early 1965

| | |
|---|---|
| 65A 2dr Hardtop | 92,705 |
| 76A Convertible | 28,833 |
| Total | 121,538 |

## Production Figures — Late 1965

| | |
|---|---|
| 63A 2dr Fastback, standard | 71,303 |
| 63B 2dr Fastback, luxury | 5,776 |
| 65A 2dr Hardtop, standard | 372,123 |
| 65B 2dr Hardtop, luxury | 22,232 |
| 65C 2dr Hardtop, bench seats | 14,905 |
| 76A Convertible, standard | 65,663 |
| 76B Convertible, luxury | 5,338 |
| 76C Convertible, bench seats | 2,111 |
| Total | 559,451 |
| Total — Early & Late | 680,989 |

## Serial Numbers

5F07F100001
5 — Last digit of model year
F — Assembly plant (F-Dearborn, R-San Jose, T-Metuchen)
07 — Plate code for 2dr Mustang (08-convertible, 09-fastback)
F — Engine code
100001 — Consecutive unit number

### Location

Stamped on driver's side inner fender panel, at notch in fender between shock tower and radiator support; warranty plate is riveted on rear face of driver's door.

### Engine Codes

U — 170 ci 1V 6 cyl 101 hp (early 1965)
T — 200 ci 1V 6 cyl 120 hp
F — 260 ci 2V V-8 164 hp (early 1965)
C — 289 ci 2V V-8 200 hp
D — 289 ci 4V V-8 210 hp (early 1965)
A — 289 ci 4V V-8 225 hp
K — 289 ci 4V V-8 271 hp high performance

## V-8 Distributors

260 ci 164 hp — C4OF-12127-A/manual, C4OF-12127-B/automatic
289 ci 200 hp — C5AF-12127-M or CZAF-12127-C or C5GF-12127-A
289 ci 210 hp —C5AF-12127-M/manual, C5AF-12127-N/automatic

## V-8 Distributors

289 ci 225 hp — C5AF-12127-M/manual,
  C5AF-12127-N/automatic
289 ci 271 hp — C30F-12127-D

## V-8 Carburetors

260 ci 164 hp — C40F-9510-A/manual, C40F-9510-B/automatic
289 ci 200 hp — C5ZF-9510-A/manual, C5ZF-9510-B or
  H/automatic
289 ci 210 hp — C4GF-9510-U/manual, C4GF-9510-E or
  V/automatic
289 ci 225 hp — C5ZF-9510-C or J/manual, C5ZF-9510-D or
  K/automatic
289 ci 271 hp — C40F-9510-AL, C50F-9510-J, L/manual
  C40F-9510-AT, C50F-9510-K, M/automatic

## Steering Gear Ratios

HCC-AT — 19.9:1
HCC-AX — 16:1
HCC-AW — 16:1

## 1965 Mustang Prices

| | Retail |
|---|---|
| Hardtop, 65A | $2,320.96 |
| Convertible, 76A | 2,557.64 |
| 2+2 Fastback, 63A | 2,533.19 |
| 200 hp 289 V-8 extra charge over 120 hp 6 cyl | 105.63 |
| 225 hp 289 V-8 extra charge over 200 hp V-8 | 52.85 |
| 271 hp 289 V-8 without GT Equipment Group | 327.92 |
| 271 hp 289 V-8 with GT Equipment Group | 276.34 |
| Cruise-O-Matic automatic transmission, 6 cyl | 175.80 |
| Cruise-O-Matic automatic transmission, 200 & 225 hp V-8s | 185.39 |
| 4-speed manual transmission, 6 cyl | 113.45 |
| 4-speed manual transmission, V-8 engines | 184.02 |
| Manual front disc brakes, 8 cyl | 56.77 |
| Limited slip differential | 41.60 |
| Rally-Pac clock/tachometer | 69.30 |
| Special Handling Package, 200 & 225 hp V-8s | 30.64 |
| GT Equipment Group | 165.03 |
| Styled steel wheels, 8 cyl only | 119.71 |
| Power brakes | 42.29 |
| Power steering | 84.47 |
| Power convertible top | 52.95 |
| Emergency flashers | 19.19 |
| Padded visors, 65A & 76A | 5.58 |
| Seatbelts, rear | 14.78 |
| Deluxe seatbelts, front (retractable) | 7.39 |
| Deluxe seatbelts, front & rear (front retractors) | 25.40 |
| Visibility Group | 35.83 |
| Accent Group, 65A & 76A | 27.11 |
| Accent Group, 63A | 13.90 |
| Air conditioner, Ford | 277.20 |

| | |
|---|---|
| Back-up lamps | 10.47 |
| Battery, heavy-duty | 7.44 |
| Closed emission system (Calif. type) | 5.19 |
| Full-length console | 50.41 |
| Console, with air conditioner | 31.52 |
| Interior Decor Group | 107.08 |
| Full-width seat (bench) with center armrest, 65A & 76A | 24.42 |
| Tinted glass with banded windshield | 30.25 |
| Windshield only, tinted & banded | 21.09 |
| Push-button radio & antenna | 57.51 |
| Rocker panel molding, 65A & 76A | 15.76 |
| Deluxe steering wheel | 31.52 |
| Vinyl roof, 65A | 74.19 |
| Wheel covers, knock-off hubs | 17.82 |
| MagicAire heater, delete (credit) | (31.52) |
| Seatbelts, delete (credit) | (10.76) |
| Tires, 6 cyl extra charge over 6.50x13 4 p.r. BSW | |
|    (5) 6.50x13 4-p.r. WSW | 33.30 |
|    (5) 6.95x14 4-p.r. BSW | 7.36 |
|    (5) 6.95x14 4-p.r. WSW | 40.67 |
| Tires, 8 cyl extra charge over 6.95x14-p.r. BSW | |
|    (5) 6.95x14 4-p.r. WSW | 33.31 |
|    (5) 6.95x14 4-p.r. BSW nylon | 15.67* |
|    (5) 6.95x14 4-p.r. WSW nylon | 48.69* |
|    (5) 6.95x14 4-p.r. Dual Red Band nylon (std. 271 hp) | 48.97 |
|   * NC with 271 hp 289 V-8 | |

## Dealer-added Accessories

| | |
|---|---|
| Door edge guards | $ 2.70 |
| Rocker panel molding (set) | 19.10 |
| Deluxe with spinner 13 in wheel covers | 28.95 |
| Deluxe with spinner 14 in wheel covers | 28.95 |
| Simulated wire 13 in wheel covers | 58.35 |
| Simulated wire 14 in wheel covers | 58.35 |
| Luggage rack | 35.00 |
| Tonneau cover, white | 52.70 |
| Tonneau cover, black | 52.70 |
| Lefthand spotlight | 29.95 |
| Vanity mirror | 1.95 |
| License plate frame | 4.50 |
| Fire extinguisher | 33.70 |
| Compass | 7.95 |
| AM radio | 53.50 |
| Rear seat speaker | 11.95 |
| Studio Sonic Sound System (Reverb) | 22.95 |
| Round (cone-shaped) outside mirror | 3.95 |
| Lefthand remote mirror | 2.25 |
| Universal (flat) outside mirror | 12.75 |
| Matching righthand mirror | 6.75 |
| Inside day-night mirror | 4.95 |
| Back-up lights | 10.40 |
| Power brakes | 47.00 |

| | |
|---|---:|
| Glovebox lock | 2.49 |
| Remote-control trunk release | 6.95 |
| Windshield washers | 14.50 |
| Rally-Pac, 6 cyl | 75.95 |
| Rally-Pac, 8 cyl | 75.95 |

## 1965 (early)
### Exterior Colors Code

| | |
|---|---|
| Raven Black | A |
| Pagoda Green | B |
| Dynasty Green | D |
| Guardsman Blue | F |
| Caspian Blue | H |
| Rangoon Red | J |
| Poppy Red | 3 |
| Silversmoke Gray | K |
| Wimbledon White | M |
| Prairie Bronze | P |
| Cascade Green | S |
| Sunlight Yellow | V |
| Vintage Burgundy | X |
| Skylight Blue | Y |
| Chantilly Beige | Z |
| Twilight Turquoise | 5 |
| Phoenician Yellow | 7 |

## 1965 (early)
### Interior Trim Code

| | |
|---|---|
| Parchment vinyl w/blue | 42 |
| Parchment vinyl w/red | 45 |
| Parchment vinyl w/black | 46 |
| Parchment vinyl w/Ivy Gold | 48 |
| White vinyl w/Palomino | 49 |
| Black vinyl & cloth | 56 |
| Blue vinyl w/blue | 82 |
| Red vinyl w/red | 85 |
| Black vinyl w/black | 86 |
| Palomino vinyl w/Palomino | 89 |

## 1965 (late)
### Exterior Colors Code

| | |
|---|---|
| Raven Black | A |
| Midnight Turquoise | B |
| Honey Gold | C |
| Dynasty Green | D |
| Caspian Blue | H |

## 1965 (late)
### Exterior Colors Code

| | |
|---|---|
| Champagne Beige | I |
| Rangoon Red | J |
| Poppy Red | 3 |
| Silversmoke Gray | K |
| Wimbledon White | M |
| Tropical Turquoise | O |
| Prairie Bronze | P |
| Ivy Green | R |
| Sunlight Yellow | V |
| Vintage Burgundy | X |
| Silver Blue | Y |
| Springtime Yellow | 8 |

## 1965 (late)
### Interior Trim Code

| | |
|---|---|
| Blue vinyl w/blue | 22 |
| Red vinyl w/red | 25 |
| Black vinyl w/black | 26 |
| Aqua | 27 |
| Ivy Gold w/gold | 28 |
| Palomino vinyl w/Palomino | 29 |
| Parchment w/blue | D2 |
| Parchment w/Burgundy | D3 |
| Parchment w/red | D5 |
| Parchment w/black | D6 |
| Parchment w/Aqua | D7 |
| Parchment w/Ivy Gold | D8 |
| Parchment w/Palomino | D9 |
| Blue & White, luxury | 62 |
| Red, luxury | 65 |
| Black, luxury | 66 |
| Aqua & white, luxury | 67 |
| Ivy Gold & white, luxury | 68 |
| Palomino, luxury | 69 |
| Parchment w/blue, luxury | F2 |
| Parchment w/Burgundy | F3 |
| Parchment w/Emberglo | F4 |

## 1965 (late)

| Interior Trim | Code |
|---|---|
| Parchment w/red, luxury | F5 |
| Parchment w/black, luxury | F6 |
| Parchment w/aqua, luxury | F7 |
| Parchment w/Ivy Gold, luxury | F8 |
| Parchment w/Palomino, luxury | F9 |
| Blue, bench | 32 |
| Red, bench | 35 |
| Black, bench | 36 |
| Palomino, bench | 39 |
| Black fabric & vinyl | 76 |
| Palomino fabric & vinyl Parchment | 79 |
| Parchment w/blue, bench | C2 |
| Parchment w/Burgundy, bench | C3 |
| Parchment w/Emberglo, bench | C4 |
| Parchment w/black, bench | C6 |
| Parchment w/Aqua, bench | C7 |
| Parchment w/Ivy Gold, bench | C8 |
| Parchment w/Palomino | C9 |

## 1965 Mustang Facts

Mustangs built between March 1964 and August 17, 1964 were known as early 1965 Mustangs. There were no 1964½ Mustangs. Those built after August 17, 1964 were known as late 1965s. A quick way to identify an early versus a late 1965 is by the electrical system. All early 1965s came with generators; late 1965s came with alternators. Generator-equipped cars came with a GEN warning light on the instrument panel; alternator-equipped Mustangs came with an ALT light. There were a multitude of other differences as well. Some worth noting are: early cars got a stationary passenger seat, a smaller handle on the automatic transmission and larger horns.

There was considerable difference between early and late 1965 Mustang engines. The base 101 hp 170 ci six-cylinder, the 164 hp 260 ci V-8 and the 210 hp 289 ci V-8 were all replaced by a 120 hp 200 ci six-cylinder, a 200 hp 289 ci V-8 and a 225 hp 289 ci V-8, respectively.

Starting in June 1964, the famous 271 hp 289 V-8 was available, and only with a four-speed manual transmission. It came with the Special Handling Package (stiffer springs, shocks and front stabilizer bar) and the fourteen-inch Red Band tires. Axle ratio choice was limited to 3.89:1 or 4.11:1. Incidentally, the Special Handling Package was available only on the 289 V-8 powered Mustangs. All Mustangs with the 271 hp 289 also came with the larger nine-inch rear axle ring gear. All other Mustangs got the smaller eight-inch rear. Only 7,273 1965 Mustangs were equipped with this engine.

The third Mustang body style, the fastback, known as the 2+2, was introduced in September 1964.

From March 1965, the Interior Decor Group, more commonly known as the Pony Interior because of the embossed ponies on the seats, became available. The letter "B" indicates this option on the body code on the warranty plate. Thus 65B, 63B and 76B all indicate the luxury interior, while the letter "A" indicates the standard interior. In addition, the Interior Decor Group option also included the five-dial instrument bezel which replaced the standard bezel.

The GT Equipment Group, available on all Mustang body styles, was available from April 1965 and only on the 225 hp and 271 hp 289 V-8 equipped Mustangs. The package consisted of manual front disc brakes, the Special Handling Package, quick ratio steering, chrome exhaust trumpets, GT emblems and rocker panel stripes, GT emblems and grille-mounted foglamps. In the interior, the standard instrument bezel was replaced with a five-dial version. As true GTs were built from February 1965 through August 1965, these Mustangs should have date codes from P to V on the warranty plate.

Only 15,079 1965 Mustangs came with the GT Equipment Group option.

The rarest 1965 Mustangs were the Indianapolis 500 Pace Car convertibles for the 1964 race. Two were used in the actual race and 35 others were given to race dignitaries. All were painted Pace Car White (which is not the same color as Wimbledon White). Additionally, 185 Indianapolis Pace Car replica hardtops were built and given to dealers. All were painted Pace Car White and equipped with the 260 ci V-8 and automatic transmission.

Two versions of the Rally-Pac clock/tachometer unit which mounted on the steering wheel were offered. The low-profile version was made to accommodate the five-dial instrument bezel that came with the Interior Decor Group and GT Equipment Group options.

Six-cylinder engines were painted red; V-8 engines were painted black with gold valve covers and air cleaners.

The Mustang lettering on the front fenders was 4⅝ inches long on early Mustangs; on later 1965s, length was increased to five inches.

Standard tires were 6.50x13 blackwalls on four- or five-lug 13x4.5 inch steel rims. Optional were whitewalls and a larger 7.00x13 size. The thirteen-inch rims were standard equipment on both six-cylinder and V-8 Mustangs, but V-8 Mustangs got five-lug rims. Optionally available were 14x4.5 inch rims with 6.50x14 tires in either four- or five-lug patterns, depending on engine. Standard with the Special Handling Package were 6.50x14 tires on five-lug 14x5.0 rims. Optional with the Special Handling Package were 15x5 inch wheels with 5.90x15 tires.

Late 1965 six-cylinder Mustangs got the same standard thirteen-inch wheels/tires, however the optional fourteen-inch size was upgraded to a 6.95x14. V-8 equipped Mustangs came with five-lug 14x5 inch wheels with the 6.95x14 tires. Standard with the Special Handling Package were 6.95x14 tires, while tires on the Hi-Po (271 hp) 289 powered Mustangs were Dual Red Line 6.95x14s. The fifteen-inch wheels/tires were dropped.

There were exhaust system variations on the 1965 Mustang. Six- and eight-cylinder single exhaust Mustangs came with a single inlet/outlet transverse-mounted muffler sandwiched between the gas tank and axle. Dual exhaust Mustangs used a transverse muffler with twin inlets/outlets plus two additional mufflers, one on each side, in front of the transverse unit. In July 1964, the factory modified the system by deleting the transverse muffler on the dual exhaust system and substituting two resonators, one on each tailpipe.

*1965 2+2*

*1965 convertible*

*1965 2+2 GT*

# Chapter 2

# 1966 Mustang

## Production Figures

| | | | |
|---|---|---|---|
| 63A 2dr Fastback, standard | 27,809 | 65C 2dr Hardtop, bench seats | 21,397 |
| 63B 2dr Fastback, luxury | 7,889 | 76A Convertible | 56,409 |
| 65A 2dr Hardtop, standard | 422,416 | 76B Convertible, luxury | 12,520 |
| 65B 2dr Hardtop, luxury | 55,938 | 76C Convertible, bench seats | 3,190 |
| | | Total | 607,568 |

## Serial Numbers

6F07C100001

6 — Last digit of model year
F — Assembly plant (F-Dearborn, R-San Jose, T-Metuchen)
07 — Plate code for 2dr Mustang (08-convertible, 09-fastback)
C — Engine code
100001 — Consecutive unit number

### Location

Stamped on driver's side inner fender panel, at notch between shock tower and radiator support; warranty plate is riveted on rear face of driver's door.

### Engine Codes

T — 200 ci 1V 6 cyl 120 hp
C — 289 ci 2V V-8 200 hp
A — 289 ci 4V V-8 225 hp
K — 289 ci 4V V-8 271 hp

## V-8 Distributors

289 ci 200 hp — C5GF-12127-A
289 ci 225 hp — C5AF-12127-M/manual, C5AF-12127-N/ automatic
289 ci 271 hp — C5OF-12127-E

## V-8 Carburetors

289 ci 200 hp — C6AF-9510-A/manual, C6AF-9510-B/automatic
289 ci 225 hp — C6ZF-9510-A,D/manual, C6ZF-9510-B,E/ automatic
289 ci 271 hp — C6ZF-9510-C/manual, C6ZF-9510-F/automatic

## Steering Gear Ratios

HCC-AT — 19.9:1
HCC-AX — 16:1
HCC-AW — 16:1

## 1966 Mustang Prices        Retail

| | |
|---|---:|
| 2dr Hardtop, 65A | $2,416.18 |
| Convertible, 76A | 2,652.86 |
| 2+2 Fastback, 63A | 2,607.07 |
| 200 hp 289 ci V–8 extra charge over 6 cyl | 105.63 |
| 225 hp 289 ci V–8 extra charge over 200 hp 289 | 52.85 |
| 271 hp 289 ci with GT Equipment Group | 276.34 |
| 271 hp 289 ci without GT Equipment Group | 327.92 |
| Cruise-O-Matic automatic transmission, 6 cyl | 175.80 |
| Cruise-O-Matic automatic transmission, 200 & 225 hp V–8s | 185.39 |
| Cruise-O-Matic automatic transmission, 271 hp V–8 | 216.27 |
| 4–speed manual transmission, 6 cyl | 113.45 |
| 4–speed manual transmission, 8 cyl | 184.02 |
| Power brakes | 42.29 |
| Power steering | 84.47 |
| Power convertible top | 52.95 |
| Air conditioner, Ford | 310.90 |
| AM Radio-Stereosonic tape system (requires radio) | 128.29 |
| Front seat, full with arm rest, 65A & 76A | 24.42 |
| Luggage rack, rear deck lid, 65A & 76A | 32.44 |
| Radio and antenna | 57.51 |
| Accent stripe, less rear quarter ornamentation | 13.90 |
| Full-length console | 50.41 |
| Console, with air conditioner | 31.52 |
| Deluxe steering wheel | 32.20 |
| Interior Decor Group | 94.13 |
| Vinyl roof, 65A | 74.36 |
| Wire wheel covers | 58.24 |
| Wheel covers, knock-off hubs | 19.48 |
| Closed crankcase emissions system | 5.19 |
| Exhaust emission control system (NA 271 hp) | 45.45 |
| MagicAire heater, delete option | (31.52) |
| Front disc brakes, 8 cyl (NA with power brakes) | 56.77 |
| Limited slip differential | 41.60 |
| Rally-Pac clock/tachometer | 69.30 |
| Special Handling Package, 200 & 225 hp V–8s | 30.64 |
| GT Equipment Group, 225 & 271 hp V–8s | 152.20 |
| Styled steel wheels, 14 in, 8 cyl only | 93.84 |
| Heavy-duty battery, 55 amp | 7.44 |
| Electric windshield wipers, 2-speed | 12.95 |
| Deluxe Seatbelts, front & rear (front retractors) and warning light | 14.53 |
| Visibility Group (remote mirror, day/nite mirror & 2-speed wipers) | 29.81 |
| Tinted glass with banded windshield | 30.25 |
| Tinted glass with windshield only | 21.09 |
| Optional tires (except with 271 hp 289) extra charge for: | |
|     (5) 6.95x14 4-p.r. WSW | 33.31 |
|     (5) 6.95x14 4-p.r. BSW nylon (NC with 271 hp) | 15.67 |
|     (5) 6.95x14 4-p.r. WSW nylon (NC with 271 hp) | 48.89 |
|     (5) 6.95x14 4-p.r. Dual Red Band nylon | 48.97 |

## 1966 Exterior Colors

| Colors | Code |
|---|---|
| Raven Black | A |
| Arcadian Blue | F |
| Sahara Beige | H |
| Nightmist Blue | K |
| Wimbledon White | M |
| Antique Bronze | P |
| Brittany Blue | Q |
| Ivy Green Metallic | R |
| Candyapple Red | T |
| Tahoe Turquoise | U |
| Emberglo | V |
| Vintage Burgundy | X |
| Silver Blue | Y |
| Sauterne Gold | Z |
| Silver Frost | 4 |
| Signalflare Red | 5 |
| Springtime Yellow | 8 |
| Dark Moss Green (late 1966) | Y7 |

Additional available colors were Medium Palomino Metallic, Medium Silver Metallic, Maroon Metallic, Silver Blue Metallic and Light Beige.

## 1966 Interior Trim

| Trim | Code |
|---|---|
| Blue w/blue | 22 |
| Dark red w/red | 25 |
| Black w/black | 26 |
| Aqua w/aqua | 27 |
| Parchment w/blue | D2 |
| Parchment w/burgundy | D3 |
| Parchment w/Emberglo | D4 |
| Parchment w/black | D6 |

## 1966 Interior Trim

| Trim | Code |
|---|---|
| Parchment w/aqua | D7 |
| Parchment w/Ivy Gold | D8 |
| Parchment w/Palomino | D9 |
| Blue & white, luxury | 62 |
| Emberglo & Parchment, luxury | 64 |
| Red, luxury | 65 |
| Black, luxury | 66 |
| Aqua & white, luxury | 67 |
| Ivy Gold & white, luxury | 68 |
| Parchment w/blue, luxury | F2 |
| Parchment w/burgundy, luxury | F3 |
| Parchment w/Emberglo, luxury | F4 |
| Parchment w/black, luxury | F6 |
| Parchment w/aqua, luxury | F7 |
| Parchment w/Ivy Gold, luxury | F8 |
| Parchment w/Palomino, luxury | F9 |
| Blue, bench | 32 |
| Red, bench | 35 |
| Black, bench | 36 |
| Parchment w/blue, bench | C2 |
| Parchment w/burgundy, bench | C3 |
| Parchment w/Ivy Gold, bench | C8 |
| Parchment w/Palomino, bench | C9 |

## 1966 Mustang Facts

The 1966 Mustangs were only slightly restyled. The most noticeable change was the floating horse in the front grille. Other changes included a redesigned gas cap, bright hood lip molding on all models, standard rocker panel moldings (except on the 2+2), standard back-up lights, redesigned side chrome spires (deleted on the GTs and those with accent pinstripes) and revised styled steel wheels. A chrome trim ring was used on the wheel, which now had only the center section chromed.

In the interior, different upholstery patterns and colors were used but the most noticeable change was the use of the five-dial instrument cluster. Padded visors were now standard equipment.

All Mustangs now came with 14x4.5 inch wheels—four lugs on six-cylinder models, five lugs with the V-8s. The standard wheel cover was redesigned. 6.95x14 was the only tire size available, with the 271 hp 289 Hi-Po engine getting premium Dual Red Band nylon tires. Whitewalls were optional.

The standard engine continued to be the 200 ci six-cylinder with the three-speed manual. The Cruise-O-Matic automatic transmission was now optional with the 271 hp "K" 289 V-8. Fewer Mustangs were equipped with this engine in 1966, only 5,469.

The GT Equipment Group still used the horizontal and vertical grille bars found on the 1965s, but did use a redesigned gas cap. The popularity of the GT option increased as 25,517 Mustangs were so equipped.

T-5 was the designation used on Mustangs exported to Germany. All Mustang emblems and names were removed as the Mustang name was used by another manufacturer there. T-5 emblems were used on both front fenders.

The Sprint 200 Option Group was available only with the 200 ci six-cylinder engine. The package, available on all three Mustang bodies, featured wire wheel covers, pinstripes, center console and a chrome air cleaner with a Sprint 200 decal. Most Sprint 200s were hardtops.

All Mustang engines were painted Ford blue.

The Mustang still used the same underdash air conditioning system. The unit's panel was painted black in 1966 and the air outlets did not have an inner trim ring.

The standard wheel cover was a slotted type with a Mustang emblem in the center.

*1966 hardtop GT*

# Chapter 3

# 1967 Mustang

## Production Figures

| | | | |
|---|---|---|---|
| 65A 2dr Hardtop | 325,853 | 76A Convertible | 38,751 |
| 65B 2dr Hardtop, luxury | 22,228 | 76B Convertible, luxury | 4,848 |
| 65C 2dr Hardtop, bench seats | 8,190 | 76C Convertible, bench seats | 1,209 |
| 63A 2dr Fastback | 53,651 | Total | 472,121 |
| 63B 2dr Fastback, luxury | 17,391 | | |

## Serial Numbers

7R01C100001

7 — Last digit of model year

R — Assembly plant (F-Dearborn, R-San Jose, T-Metuchen)

01 — Plate code for 2dr hardtop (02-fastback, 03-convertible)

C — Engine code

100001 — Consecutive unit number

### Location

Stamped on driver's side inner fender panel, at notch between shock tower and radiator support; warranty plate is riveted on rear face of driver's door.

### Engine Codes

U — 200 ci 1V 6 cyl 120 hp

C — 289 ci 2V V-8 200 hp

A — 289 ci 4V V-8 225 hp

K — 289 ci 4V V-8 271 hp

S — 390 ci 4V V-8 320 hp

## V-8 Distributors

289 ci 200 hp — C7OF-12127-A, B, D or E

289 ci 225 hp — C5AF-12127-M/manual, C5AF-12127-N/automatic

289 ci 271 hp — C50F-12127-E

390 ci 320 hp — C7AF-12127-U/non-Thermactor, -F/with Thermactor

## V-8 Carburetors

289 ci 200 hp — C7DF-9510-E, G/manual, C7DF-9510-F, H, N, V/automatic

289 ci 225 hp — C7DF-9510-L, C/manual, C7DF-9510-M, D/automatic

289 ci 271 hp — C6ZF-9510-C/manual, C6ZF-9510-C/automatic

390 ci 320 hp — C7OF-9510-A, C (Holley R-3795)/manual, C7OF-9510-B, D, (Holley R-3796)/automatic

## Steering Gear Ratios

SMB-A — 19.9:1
SMB-B — 16:1
SMB-C — 19.9:1
SMB-D — 19.9:1
SMB-E — 16:1

| 1967 Mustang Prices | Retail |
|---|---|
| 2dr Hardtop, 65A | $2,461.46 |
| Convertible, 76A | 2,698.14 |
| 2+2 Fastback, 63A | 2,592.17 |
| 289 ci 200 hp V-8 | 105.63 |
| 289 ci 225 hp V-8 | 158.48 |
| 289 ci 271 hp V-8 (with GT Equipment Group only) | 433.55 |
| 390 ci 320 hp V-8 | 263.71 |
| Cruise-O-Matic automatic transmission, 6 cyl | 188.18 |
| Cruise-O-Matic automatic transmission, 200 or 225 hp V-8 | 197.89 |
| Cruise-O-Matic automatic transmission, 271 or 320 hp | 220.17 |
| 4-speed manual transmission, 200 & 225 hp V-8 | 184.02 |
| 4-speed manual transmission, 271 & 320 hp V-8 | 233.18 |
| Heavy-duty 3-speed manual, required with 320 hp V-8 | 79.20 |
| Power front disc brakes | 64.77 |
| Power steering | 84.47 |
| Power convertible top | 52.95 |
| GT Equipment Group (with V-8s only) | 205.05 |
| Limited slip differential | 41.60 |
| Styled steel wheels (2+2 only) | 93.84 |
| Styled steel wheels, all others | 115.11 |
| Competition handling package (with GT Equip. only) | 388.53 |
| Tinted windows and windshield | 30.25 |
| Convenience Control Panel | 39.50 |
| Fingertip speed control (requires V-8 & Cruise-O-Matic) | 71.30 |
| Remote control outside mirror (std. 2+2) | 9.58 |
| Convertible safety glass rear window | 32.44 |
| SelectAire air conditioner | 356.09 |
| AM push-button radio | 57.51 |
| AM/FM push-button radio | 133.65 |
| Stereosonic tape system (AM radio required) | 128.49 |
| 2+2 folding rear seat and access door (Sport Deck option) | 64.77 |
| Full-width front seat (NA 2+2) | 24.42 |
| Tilt-away steering wheel | 59.93 |
| Rear deck luggage rack (2+2) | 32.44 |
| Comfortweave vinyl trim (NA convertible) | 24.53 |
| Center console (requires radio) | 50.41 |
| Deluxe steering wheel | 31.52 |
| Exterior decor group | 38.86 |
| Lower back panel grille | 19.48 |
| Interior Decor Group (convertible) | 94.36 |
| Interior Decor Group (all others) | 108.06 |
| Two-tone paint (lower back grille) | 12.95 |
| Accent paint stripe | 13.90 |
| Vinyl-covered roof (hardtop) | 74.36 |
| Wheel covers (std. 2+2) | 21.34 |

| | |
|---|---:|
| Wire wheel covers (2+2) | 58.24 |
| Wire wheel covers (all others) | 79.51 |
| Wide Oval Sports tires (V-8 required) | 62.35 |
| Whitewall tire option (typical) | 33.31 |
| Rocker panel molding (std. 2+2) | 15.59 |
| MagicAire heater (delete option) | (31.52) |

| 1967 Exterior Colors | Code | 1967 Interior Trim | Code |
|---|---|---|---|
| Raven Black | A | Black | 2A |
| Frost Turquoise | B | Blue | 2B |
| Acapulco Blue | D | Red | 2D |
| Arcadian Blue | F | Saddle | 2F |
| Diamond Green | H | Ivy Gold | 2G |
| Lime Gold | I | Aqua | 2K |
| Nightmist Blue | K | Parchment | 2U |
| Wimbledon White | M | Black, luxury | 6A |
| Diamond Blue | N | Blue, luxury | 6B |
| Brittany Blue | Q | Red, luxury | 6D |
| Dusk Rose | S | Saddle, luxury | 6F |
| Candyapple Red | T | Ivy Gold, luxury | 6G |
| Burnt Amber | V | Aqua, luxury | 6K |
| Clearwater Aqua | W | Parchment, luxury | 6U |
| Vintage Burgundy | X | Black, bench seat | 4A |
| Dark moss Green | Y | Parchment, bench seat | 4U |
| Sauterne Gold | Z | Black comfortweave | 7A |
| Silver Frost | 4 | Parchment comfortweave | 7U |
| Pebble Beige | 6 | Black comfortweave, luxury | 5A |
| Springtime Yellow | 8 | Parchment comfortweave, luxury | 5U |

Additional special 1967 colors were Playboy Pink, Anniversary Gold, Columbine Blue, Aspen Gold, Blue Bonnet, Timberline Green, Lavender and Bright Red.

## Convertible Top Colors
Black or White

## 1967 Mustang Facts

The Mustang was completely redesigned for 1967. It was longer and wider, but it did have the same 108 inch wheelbase of its predecessor. The grille opening was enlarged for a decidedly meaner look, while the rear taillight panel was concave. The fastback became a full fastback, and simulated rear quarter panel scoops were used on all three body styles.

The front suspension was widened and redesigned which resulted in a better ride. The optional front disc brakes came with power assist, and the 1967 Mustang was the first to use a dual hydraulic brake system.

Engine selection remained the same as in 1966, but with one major exception. The 390 ci big block, rated at 320 hp, brought serious performance to the Mustang. The 390 used cast iron intake and exhaust manifolds. Carburetion was a single 600 cfm Holley four-barrel. All 390s installed in the Mustang used a dual exhaust system. A total of 28,800 Mustangs were equipped with the 390. The previous hotshot, the 271 hp 289 V-8, saw its popularity wane, as only 472 were built. The GT Equipment Group option was mandatory with the 271 hp 289.

The premier performance Mustang was still the GT. The GT Equipment Group consisted of the grille-mounted foglamps, power front disc brakes, dual exhausts with chrome quad outlets (excluded on the 200 hp 289), F70x14 tires, GT gas cap, the handling package, rocker panel stripes, and GT or GTA (for automatic transmission equipped GTs) emblems. A total of 24,079 Mustangs were equipped with the GT option.

Available only with the GT Equipment Group was the Competition Handling Package, consisting of firmer suspension components, limited slip rear axle and fifteen-inch wheels with wire wheel covers.

The interior was also redesigned. Most noticeable was the new dash, which did away with the Rally-Pac and also featured integral air conditioning. The Tilt-away steering wheel was a new option, as was the fold-down rear seat on the fastback. Other new options included cruise control, a folding glass rear window on the convertibles and an Exterior Decor Group which included a hood with rear-facing louvers that housed turn signal indicators, wheelwell moldings and a pop-open gas cap.

The Interior Decor Group option did not include the galloping Pony inserts.

The Convenience Control Panel housed four warning lights and was located on the dash above the radio (without A/C). With A/C the panel was available only in conjunction with the console. Lights in this case were mounted on either side of the storage compartment. The four lights were: parking brake warning light, door ajar, seatbelt reminder and low fuel.

Standard wheel cover was a 10½ inch hubcap or a 21-spoke wheel cover.

The optional styled steel wheels were wider, necessitating a wider trim ring, and used a blue center cap.

The Dagenham four-speed manual transmission, previously used with the 200 ci six-cylinder, was no longer available.

As with previous Mustangs, there was a long list of dealer-installed options which included the Cobra kits. With these kits, the Mustang enthusiast could improve performance from mild to wild.

Vinyl roof colors were limited to two: black or parchment.

1967 Mustangs used polyethylene-filled ball joints. Manual steering ratio was reduced from a super slow 27:1 to an almost super slow 25.3:1. Power steering ratio was 20.3:1.

*1967 convertible*

*1967 Fastback GT*

# Chapter 4

# 1968 Mustang

## Production Figures

| | | | |
|---|---|---|---|
| 63A 2dr Fastback | 33,585 | 65C 2dr Hardtop, | |
| 63B 2dr Fastback | | bench seats | 6,113 |
| Deluxe | 7,661 | 65D 2dr Hardtop | |
| 63C 2dr Fastback, | | Deluxe, bench seats | 853 |
| bench seats | 1,079 | 76A Convertible | 22,037 |
| 63D 2dr Fastback | | 76B Convertible | |
| Deluxe, bench seats | 256 | Deluxe | 3,339 |
| 65A 2dr Hardtop | 233,472 | Total | 317,404 |
| 65B 2dr Hardtop | | | |
| Deluxe | 9,009 | | |

## Serial Numbers

8R01J100001

8 — Last digit of model year
R — Assembly plant (F-Dearborn, R-San Jose, T-Metuchen)
01 — Plate code for 2dr hardtop (02-fastback, 03-convertible)
J — Engine code
100001 — Consecutive unit number

### Location

Stamped on plate riveted on passenger's side of instrument panel, visible through the windshield; also stamped on left inner fender; warranty plate is riveted on rear face of driver's door.

### Engine Codes

T — 200 ci 1V 6 cyl 120 hp
C — 289 ci 2V V-8 195 hp
F — 302 ci 2V V-8 210 hp
J — 302 ci 4V V-8 230 hp
S — 390 ci 4V V-8 325 hp
W — 427 ci 4V V-8 390 hp
R — 428 ci 4V V-8 335 hp (Cobra Jet)

## V-8 Distributors

289 ci 195 hp — C8TF-12127-F/manual,
    C8OF-12127-C/automatic
302 ci 210 hp — C8AF-12127-E/manual,
    C8OF-12127-C/automatic
302 ci 230 hp — C8ZF-12127-A/manual,
    C8ZF-12127-D/automatic
390 ci 325 hp — C7OF-12127-H
427 ci 390 hp — C7OF-12127-F
428 ci 335 hp — C8OF-12127-H/manual,
    C8OF-12127-J/automatic

## V-8 Carburetors
289 ci 195 hp — C8AF-9510-AF/manual,
C8OF-9510-S/automatic
302 ci 210 hp — C8AF-9510-AK/manual,
C8AF-9510-AL/automatic
302 ci 230 hp — C8ZF-9510-A, C or D/manual,
C8ZF-9510-B or D/automatic
390 ci 325 hp — C8OF-9510-C(Holley R-3795)/manual,
C8OF-9510-D(Holley R-3796)/automatic
427 ci 390 hp — C8AF-9510-AD(Holley R-4088)
428 ci 335 hp — C8OF-9510-AA(Holley R-4168)/manual,
C8OF-9510-AB(Holley R-4174)/automatic

## Steering Gear Ratios
SMB-D — 19.9:1
SMB-F — 19.9:1
SMB-K — 16:1

| 1968 Mustang Prices | Retail |
|---|---|
| 2door Hardtop, 63A | $2,578.60 |
| Convertible | 2,814.22 |
| 2+2 Fastback | 2,689.26 |
| 289 ci 195 hp V-8 | 105.63 |
| 302 ci 230 hp V-8 | 171.77 |
| 390 ci 325 hp V-8 | 263.71 |
| 427 ci 390 hp V-8 | 622.00 |
| 428 ci 335 hp V-8* | 434.00 |
| SelectShift Cruise-O-Matic, 6 cyl | 191.12 |
| SelectShift Cruise-O-Matic, 195/230 hp V-8s | 200.85 |
| SelectShift Cruise-O-Matic, 325 hp V-8 | 233.17 |
| 4-speed manual transmission, 195/230 hp V-8s | 184.02 |
| 4-speed manual transmission, 325 hp V-8 | 233.18 |
| Power front disc brakes, V-8s (required with 325hp V-8 on GT Equipment Group) | 64.77 |
| Power steering | 84.47 |
| Power convertible top | 52.95 |
| Convertible glass backlite | 38.86 |
| GT Equipment Group, 230/325 hp V-8 (NA with Sports Trim Group or optional wheel covers) | 146.71 |
| Tachometer (V-8s only) | 54.45 |
| Limited slip differential | 41.60 |
| Tinted windows and windshield | 30.25 |
| Convenience Group (console required with SelectAire) | 32.44 |
| Fingertip speed control (with V-8 and SelectShift) | 73.83 |
| Remote control outside mirror, lefthand side | 9.58 |
| SelectAire air conditioner | 360.30 |
| Push-button radio (AM) | 61.40 |
| AM/FM stereo radio | 181.39 |
| Stereosonic tape system (AM radio required) | 133.86 |
| Sport Deck rear seat (2+2 only) | 64.77 |
| Full-width front seat (hardtop & 2+2, NA console) | 32.44 |
| Tilt-away steering wheel | 66.14 |

| | |
|---|---|
| Center console (radio required) | 53.71 |
| Interior Decor Group (convertible & full-width front seat) | 110.16 |
| Interior Decor Group (all others without full-width seat) | 123.86 |
| Two-tone hood paint | 19.48 |
| Accent paint stripe | 13.90 |
| Vinyl-covered roof (hardtop only) | 74.36 |
| Wheel covers (NA with GT or V-8 Sports Trim Groups) | 21.34 |
| Deluxe wheel covers (NA with GT or V-8 Sports Trim Groups) | 34.33 |
| Wide Oval tire option (V-8s only) | 78.53 |
| Whitewall tire option | 33.31 |

*Available after April 1, 1968

## 1968 Exterior Colors

| | Code |
|---|---|
| Raven Black | A |
| Royal Maroon | B |
| Acapulco Blue | D |
| Gulfstream Aqua | F |
| Lime Gold | I |
| Wimbledon White | M |
| Diamond Blue | N |
| Seafoam Green | O |
| Brittany Blue | Q |
| Highland Green | R |
| Candyapple Red | T |
| Tahoe Turquoise | U |
| Meadowlark Yellow | W |
| Presidential Blue | X |
| Sunlit Gold | Y |
| Pebble Beige | 6 |

## 1968 Interior Trim

| | Code* |
|---|---|
| Black vinyl | 2A(6A) |
| Blue vinyl | 2B(6B) |
| Dark red vinyl | 2D(6D) |
| Saddle vinyl | 2F(6F) |
| Ivy Gold vinyl | 2G(6G) |

## 1968 Interior Trim

| | Code* |
|---|---|
| Aqua vinyl | 2K(6K) |
| Parchment vinyl | 2U(6U) |
| Nugget Gold vinyl | 2Y(6Y) |
| Black comfortweave, bench | 8A(9A) |
| Blue comfortweave, bench | 8B(9B) |
| Dark red comfortweave, bench | 8D(9D) |
| Parchment comfortweave, bench | 8U(9U) |
| Black comfortweave | 7A(5A) |
| Blue comfortweave | 7B(5B) |
| Dark red comfortweave | 7D(5D) |
| Parchment comfortweave | 8U(5U) |

*Parentheses indicates with Decor Group

## Convertible Top Colors

Black or White

## 1968 Mustang Facts

The 289 ci 225 hp V-8 was replaced by a 302 ci rated at 230 hp. Increased displacement was achieved by increasing the stroke on the 289 from 2.87 inches to 3.00 inches. The two-barrel carburetor 289 (rated at 195 hp for 1968) was replaced mid-year by a two-barrel 302 rated at 210 hp. Thus both 289- and 302-powered Mustangs were available in 1968.

The base engine, the 200 ci six-cylinder, remained unchanged while the 390 ci V-8 was rated at 325 hp, an increase of five hp. Top engine option was a Low Riser version of Ford's famous 427 ci V-8. Featuring a Holley 600 cfm carburetor and available only with an automatic transmission, it was rated at 390 hp. A rare and expensive option, it was deleted from the option list in December 1967. Look for the letter "W" in the VIN for engine code.

A total of 11,475 1968 Mustangs were equipped with the 390 ci V-8.

On April 1, 1968 Ford introduced a special version of the 428 ci V-8 for use in the Mustang, known as the 428 Cobra Jet. The 428 Cobra Jet was basically a production 428 fitted with 427 Low Riser heads, but with a host of improvements. Rated at 335 hp, it actually produced more than 400. Available only with the GT Equipment Group, 428 CJ Mustangs also came with functional Ram Air hood scoop, power front disc brakes and staggered rear shocks for four-speed transmission cars. The C-6 three-speed automatic was also available. A total of 2,253 fastbacks and 564 hardtops were built. An unknown small number of convertibles were built as well.

Goodyear Polyglas F70x14 tires made their debut on the 428CJ Mustangs.

The horizontal grille bars were deleted on 1968 Mustangs and on the GT Mustangs as well. Due to governmental regulations, all Mustangs came with front and rear quarter panel reflectors. Mustangs built before February 15, 1968 came with a rectangular rear reflector while those built after had a bolt-on reflector with oval chrome trim. All 1968 Mustangs came with chrome rocker panel moldings. The simulated side scoops of 1967 were replaced by a vertical ornament.

Two-tone painted louvered hoods were optional on all Mustangs.

The GT Equipment Group was still available on the 230/325/390 hp Mustangs. Differences from the previous year were the new 14-inch styled steel wheels (chromed or painted argent) with GT hubcaps, a new pop-open GT gas cap, new side "C" stripes and new quarter panel GT emblems. There was no separate GTA designation to differentiate automatic-transmission-equipped GTs. GT production dropped to 17,458 in 1968.

The Sprint option package on six-cylinder Mustangs included GT side stripes, pop-open gas cap and full wheel covers. The V-8 Sprint option added GT foglamps and the styled steel wheels with the Wide Oval tires.

The California Special GT/CS was a special trim package available on hardtops in California only. It used a Shelby rear deck lid with integral spoiler and sequential taillights and Shelby non-functional side scoops. The Mustang ornament was deleted from the blacked-out grille opening. Special side stripes, styled steel wheels and Lucas or Marchal foglamps completed the package. About 5,000 were built.

Similar to the California Special was the High Country Special, this time sold only by Colorado dealers. Identical to the GT/CS, with the exception of the High Country Special decal taking the place of the GT/CS identification on the side scoops, the High Country Specials had been available in Colorado since 1966. The only difference from regular production Mustangs was the addition of the High Country Special decal.

The Mustang Sprint option consisted of GT stripes, pop-open gas cap and full wheel covers on six-cylinder Mustangs. V-8s got, in addition, the styled steel wheels with Wide Oval tires and the GT foglamps.

The rear taillight bezels on 1968 Mustangs are painted black, versus chrome on the 1967s.

The Reflective Group, optional on GT-equipped Mustangs, consisted of reflective GT side stripes and reflective paint on the wheels.

The Sports Trim Group consisted of woodgrain dash panel applique, knitted inserts in the bucket seats (hardtops and fastbacks) bright wheelwell moldings, two-tone louvered hood and, on V-8s only, argent styled steel wheels with E70x14 tires.

The primary difference between 1967 and 1968 Interior Decor Groups was the use of woodgrain dash appliques in 1968. The steering wheel center was redesigned for 1968, using a wide two-spoke center section.

1968 bucket seats have locking seat backs. A chrome lever is used to unlock the seat.

The collapsible spare tire was optional for the first time in 1968, as were front headrests.

Beginning with 1968, the disc brakes used on Mustangs have a single piston floating caliper.

*1968 Fastback GT*

# Chapter 5

# 1969 Mustang

## Production Figures

| | | | |
|---|---|---|---|
| 63A 2dr Fastback | 56,022 | 65E 2dr Hardtop | |
| 63B 2dr Fastback | | Grande | 22,182 |
| Deluxe | 5,958 | 76A Convertible | 11,307 |
| 63C 2dr Fastback | | 76B Convertible | |
| Mach 1 | 72,458 | Deluxe | 3,439 |
| 65A 2dr Hardtop | 118,613 | Total | 299,824 |
| 65B 2dr Hardtop | | | |
| Deluxe | 5,210 | **Specials** (included in above | |
| 65C 2dr Hardtop, | | figures) | |
| bench seats | 4,131 | Boss 302 | 1,628 |
| 65D 2dr Hardtop | | Boss 429 | 859 |
| Deluxe, bench seats | 504 | (includes two Boss Cougars) | |

## Serial Numbers

9F02Z100001

9 — Last digit of model year
F — Assembly plant (F-Dearborn, R-San Jose, T-Metuchen)
02 — Plate code for Mustang fastback (01-hardtop, 03-convertible)
Z — Engine code
100001 — Consecutive unit number

### Location

Stamped on plate riveted on driver's side of instrument panel, visible through the windshield; stamped on left inner fender; warranty plate is riveted on rear face of driver's door.

### Engine Codes

T — 200 ci 1V 6 cyl 115 hp
L — 250 ci 1V 6 cyl 155 hp
F — 302 ci 2V V-8 220 hp
G — 302 ci 4V V-8 (Boss) 290 hp
H — 351 ci 2V V-8 250 hp
M — 351 ci 4V V-8 290 hp
S — 390 ci 4V V-8 320 hp
Q — 428 ci 4V V-8 (CJ) 335 hp
R — 428 ci 4V V-8 (CJ-R) 335 hp
Z — 429 ci 4V V-8 (Boss) 375 hp

## V-8 Distributors

302 ci 220 hp — C8AF-12127-E/manual,
    C8OF-12127-C/automatic
302 ci 290 hp — C9ZF-12127-F
351 ci 250 hp — C9OF-12127-M, N/manual, C9OF-12127-M,
    T/automatic

351 ci 290 hp — C9OF-12127-M, N/manual, C9OF-12127-M, T/automatic
390 ci 320 hp — C9AF-12127-K/manual, C7AF-12127-AC/automatic
428 ci 335 hp — C8OF-12127-H/manual, C8OF-12127-J/automatic
429 ci 375 hp — C9ZF-12127-U, D

## V-8 Carburetors
302 ci 220 hp — C8AF-9510-BD/manual, C9AF-9510-A/automatic
302 ci 290 hp — C9ZF-9510-J(Holley R-4511)
351 ci 250 hp — C9ZF-9510-A/manual, C9ZF-9510-B/automatic
351 ci 290 hp — C9ZF-9510-C/manual, C9ZF-9510-D/automatic
390 ci 320 hp — C9ZF-9510-E/manual, C9ZF-9510-F/automatic
428 ci 335 hp — C9AF-9510-M(Holley R-4279)/manual, C9AF-9510-H(Holley R-4280)/automatic
429 ci 375 hp — C9AF-9510-S(Holley R-4456)

## Steering Gear Ratios
SMB-D — 19.9:1
SMB-F — 16:1
SMB-K — 16:1

| 1969 Mustang Prices | Retail |
| --- | --- |
| Hardtop, 65A | $2,618.00 |
| Convertible, 76A | 2,832.00 |
| SportsRoof, 63A | 2,618.00 |
| Mach 1, 63C | 3,122.00 |
| Grande, 65E | 2,849.00 |
| 250 ci 155 hp 6 cyl (NA Mach 1) | 25.91 |
| 302 ci 220 hp V-8 (NA Mach 1) | 105.00 |
| Extra charge over 302 ci V-8 for: | |
| 351 ci 250 hp V-8 (std. Mach 1) | 58.34 |
| 351 ci 290 hp V-8 (except Mach 1) | 84.25 |
| Mach 1 over 351 ci 250 hp | 25.91 |
| 390 ci 320 hp V-8 (except Mach 1) | 158.08 |
| Mach 1 over 351 ci 250 hp | 99.74 |
| 428 ci 335 hp V-8 (except Mach 1) | 287.53 |
| Mach 1 over 351 ci 250 hp | 224.12 |
| 428 ci 335 hp Ram Air Cobra Jet (CJ-R) V-8 (except Mach 1) | 420.96 |
| Mach 1 over 351 ci 250 hp | 357.46 |
| Boss 302 ci 4V 8 cyl engine | 676.15 |
| 429 ci 4V Cobra Jet HO (Boss 429) | 1208.35 |
| SelectShift transmission, 6 cyl | 191.13 |
| 302 & 351 ci V-8s | 200.85 |
| 390 & 428 ci V-8s | 222.08 |
| 4-speed manual transmission, 302 & 351 ci V-8s | 204.64 |
| 4-speed manual transmission, 390 & 428 ci V-8s | 253.92 |
| Power front disc brake (NA 200 ci 6 cyl) | 64.77 |
| Power steering | 94.95 |

| | |
|---|---|
| Power convertible top | 52.95 |
| Convertible glass rear window | 38.86 |
| GT Equipment Group (NA Grande, 6 cyl or 302 V-8) | 146.71 |
| Tachometer (V-8 only) | 54.45 |
| Limited slip differential, 250 & 302 V-8 | 41.60 |
| Traction-Lok differential (NA 6 cyl & 302 V-8) | 63.51 |
| Optional axle ratio | 6.53 |
| Intermittent windshield wipers | 16.85 |
| High-back bucket seats (NA Grande) | 84.25 |
| Color-keyed racing mirrors | 19.48 |
| Handling suspension (NA Grande or W200, 250 & 428) | 30.64 |
| Competition Suspension (428 only, std. Mach 1) | 30.64 |
| Power ventilation (NA w/SelectAire) | 40.02 |
| Electric clock (std. Mach 1, Grande) | 15.59 |
| Tinted windshield & windows | 32.44 |
| Speed control (V-8 & SelectShift) | 73.83 |
| Remote control outside mirror, lefthand | 12.95 |
| SelectAire air conditioner (NA 200 ci & 428 ci with | |
|     4-speed manual) | 379.57 |
| Push-button AM radio | 61.40 |
| AM/FM stereo radio | 181.36 |
| Stereosonic tape (AM radio required) | 133.84 |
| Rear seat speaker (hardtop & Grande) | 12.95 |
| Rear seat deck (SportsRoof & Mach 1) | 97.21 |
| Full-width front seat (hardtop, NA console) | 32.44 |
| Tilt-away steering wheel | 66.14 |
| Rim Blow deluxe steering wheel | 35.70 |
| Console | 53.82 |
| Interior Decor Group (NA Mach 1, Grande) | 101.10 |
|     with color-keyed mirror option | 88.15 |
| Deluxe Interior Decor Group (SportsRoof & conv.) | 133.44 |
|     with color-keyed mirror option | 120.48 |
| Deluxe seatbelts with warning light | 15.59 |
| Vinyl-covered roof (Grande & hardtop) | 84.25 |
| Wheel covers (NA Mach 1, GT, Grande, std. | |
|     Exterior Decor Group) | 21.38 |
| Wire wheel covers (std. Grande, NA Mach 1, GT Group) | 79.51 |
| Wire wheel covers (Exterior Decor Group) | 58.27 |
| Exterior Decor Group (NA Mach 1, Grande) | 32.44 |
| Chrome styled steel wheels (std. Mach 1, NA Grande | |
|     & 200 ci 6 cyl) | 116.59 |
|     with GT Group | 77.73 |
|     with Exterior Decor Group | 95.31 |
| Adjustable head restraints (NA Mach 1) | 17.00 |
| Visibility Group | 11.16 |
| Functional adjustable rear spoiler (Boss 302) | 19.48 |
| Sport Slats (Boss 302) | 128.28 |
| Trunk-mounted 85 amp battery (Boss 429) | 32.44 |
| Functional front air spoiler (Boss 429) | 13.05 |
| Shaker hood scoop (351 & 390 engines) | 84.25 |

## 1969 Exterior Colors

| Colors | Code |
|---|---|
| Raven Black | A |
| Royal Maroon | B |
| Black Jade | C |
| Acapulco Blue | D |
| Aztec Aqua | E |
| Gulfstream Aqua | F |
| Lime Gold | I |
| Wimbledon White | M |
| Winter Blue | P |
| Champagne Gold | S |
| Candyapple Red | T |
| Meadowlark Yellow | W |
| Indian Fire Red | Y |
| New Lime | 2 |
| Calypso Coral | 3 |
| Silver Jade | 4 |
| Pastel Grey | 6 |

## 1969 Interior Trim

| Trim | Code* |
|---|---|
| Black vinyl | 2A |
| Blue vinyl | 2B |
| Red vinyl | 2D |
| Ivy Gold vinyl | 2G |
| Nugget Gold vinyl | 2Y |
| Black comfortweave, high buckets | 4A(DA) |
| Red comfortweave, high buckets | 4D(DD) |
| White comfortweave, high buckets | (DW) |
| Black comfortweave, luxury | 5A |
| Blue comfortweave, luxury | 5B |
| Red comfortweave, luxury | 5D |
| Ivy Gold comfortweave, luxury | 5G |

## 1969 Interior Trim

| Trim | Code* |
|---|---|
| White comfortweave, luxury | 5W |
| Nugget Gold comfortweave, luxury | 5Y |
| Black comfortweave, bench | 8A(9A) |
| Blue comfortweave, bench | 8B(9B) |
| Red comfortweave, bench | 8D(9D) |
| Nugget Gold comfortweave, bench | 8Y(9Y) |
| Black, convertible | 7A |
| Blue convertible, deluxe | 7B |
| Red convertible, deluxe | 7D |
| Ivy Gold convertible, deluxe | 7G |
| White convertible, deluxe | 7W |
| Nugget Gold convertible, deluxe | 7Y |
| Black cloth & vinyl, luxury | 1A |
| Blue cloth & vinyl, luxury | 1B |
| Ivy Gold cloth & vinyl, luxury | 1G |
| Nugget Gold cloth & vinyl, luxury | 1Y |
| Black, Mach 1 | 3A |
| Red, Mach 1 | 3D |
| White, Mach 1 | 3W |

*Parentheses indicates Interior Decor Group

## Convertible Top Colors

Black or White

# 1969 Mustang Facts

1969 was the second major restyle for the Mustang. Every dimension increased with the exception of wheelbase (it remained at 108 inches) and height, which was lowered by 1½ inches.

Including the two Boss engines, there was a total of ten different engines available.

Headlight configuration for the first time went to four, four-inch units. The fastback body style, called SportsRoof, came with simulated rear side scoops and a spoilered rear. Convertibles and hardtops used a simulated rear quarter panel vent.

The interior was totally restyled, with two separate dash pods available. The standard driver's side pod housed, from left to right, alternator, speedometer, a combination of fuel and temperature, and oil pressure. If the optional tachometer was ordered, it took the place of the fuel and temperature gauges. The temperature gauge was relocated to the far left, displacing the alternator gauge, while the temperature gauge displaced the oil pressure gauge on the far right.

The Deluxe Interior Group (standard on Mach 1, Grande and Boss 429) came with simulated woodgrain appliques on the dash, door panels and console. A clock was also housed on the passenger side dash pod. Numerals on the speedometer (and optional tachometer) were smaller than the standard interior's and the speedometer was divided in multiples of five. Instrument face color with the Deluxe Interior Group was dark grey, versus black for standard. This interior was optional only on SportsRoofs and hardtops.

The Interior Decor Group consisted of the molded door panels with woodgrain applique, comfortweave buckets, the Deluxe three-spoke Rim Blow steering wheel and a driver's side remote rectangular mirror. The high-back bucket seats were optional with either interior option.

1969 was the last year that bench seats were available and only on the hardtops. Also in 1969, the dual color-keyed race-type mirrors were optional on all Mustangs.

The Exterior Decor Group consisted of rocker panel moldings, wheelwell and rear end moldings.

The GT Equipment Group was still available on all three body styles as long as the engine was 351 ci or larger. It consisted of rocker panel GT stripes, GT gas cap, GT hubcaps on styled steel wheels, pin-type hood latches, heavy-duty suspension, simulated hood scoop and chrome quad outlets with dual-exhaust-equipped engines. Only 5,396 Mustangs got this option.

New engines included a 155 hp 250 ci six-cylinder, on which air conditioning was available. Two 351 ci V-8s, basically stretched 302s, joined the lineup. The two-barrel version was rated at 250 hp while the four-barrel was rated 290 hp. These engines were built at Ford's Windsor plant and thus are known as the 351 Windsor or 351W. The 390 was still available, but with a 470 cfm Ford carburetor rather than the previous Holley. A total of 10,494 Mustangs came with the 390.

The 428 Cobra Jet was the top production engine option. Two versions were available, both rated at 335 hp. The non-Ram Air version had the letter "Q" for its engine code, while those equipped with the functional Shaker hood scoop had the letter "R." The optional four-speed manual that was available with the 428CJ was the close ratio version, with a 2.32:1 first gear. All 428s also came with the larger 31 spline rear. 13,193 1969 Mustangs came with the 428CJ.

If a 3.91:1 (code V) or 4.30:1 (code W) rear axle ratio was ordered, the 428CJ was automatically upgraded to Super Cobra Jet (SCJ) status. These engines used special capscrew 427 LeMans type connecting rods, different crankshaft, flywheel and damper, and an external oil cooler mounted in front of the radiator, which reduced oil temperature by 30 degrees. All this for $6.53—without a doubt the best value option of the year.

Service bulletins on the 428CJ specified that an additional quart of oil be added during an oil change, for a total of six quarts.

The Grande Mustang was a luxury version of the Mustang hardtop. Standard equipment was the Deluxe Decor Group, wire wheel covers, color-keyed dual mirrors, two-tone paint stripes and Grande lettering on each C pillar.

The rare Mustang E was a specially equipped Mustang Sports-Roof designed for economy. It came with the 250 ci six-cylinder, high stall torque converter automatic transmission and a very low, 2.33:1 rear axle ratio. Mustang E lettering on the rear quarters identified the Mustang as such.

The Mach 1 took the place of the GT as the premier performance Mustang. It was based on the SportsRoof and came with a long list of standard features. The hood was painted flat black along with a similarly painted non-functional hood scoop. Reflective side and rear stripes were coordinated to complement the body color, as were color-keyed dual racing mirrors. Adding to the racer image were the NASCAR hood pin latches—a deleteable option. Chrome styled steel wheels and a chrome pop-open gas cap were also used. The Deluxe Decor Group was used in the interior. Standard engine was the 351-2V. The optional 4V engines came with chrome quad outlets. The Competition Suspension was standard equipment and included staggered rear shocks with the four-speed 428CJs.

Standard tires on the Mach 1 were E70x14s. F70x14 RWL Polyglas tires were mandatory with the 428s.

The Shaker scoop was optional on 351-2V, 351-4V and 390 engines. It was standard with the 428CJ-R.

The limited production Boss 302 was based on the SportsRoof body, but without the simulated side scoops. Flat black paint was used on the hood, headlight buckets, rear deck and taillight panels. A large C side stripe with Boss 302 lettering was used on the sides. Colors were limited to just four: Wimbledon White, Bright Yellow, Calypso Coral and Acapulco Blue. Most Boss 302s came with the standard black Mustang interior, though other colors were optional. A front chin spoiler was standard, while the rear window Sport Slats and rear wing were options. The rear spoiler was plastic on the 1969 Boss 302.

Standard wheels were argent painted 15x7 Magnum 500s using Goodyear F60x15 Polyglas tires. Chrome Magnum 500s were optional. All four fenders on the Boss 302 were radiused so that the tires would not hit.

The Boss 302 engine block was a special strengthened four-bolt main version of the production 302. It used forged steel connecting rods, a forged steel crank and special cylinder heads utilizing 2.23-inch (intake) and 1.72-inch (exhaust) valves. An aluminum high-rise intake manifold and a Holley 780 cfm carburetor provided induction. All Boss 302 engines came with a mechanical lifter camshaft and a dual-point distributor. All Boss 302s came with a four-speed wide ratio (2.78:1 first gear) manual transmission.

Other standard Boss 302 features were front disc brakes, quick ratio (16:1) steering, 3.50:1 rear axle ratio and staggered rear shocks.

The Boss 302's consecutive unit number was stamped on the engine block (at the rear center on a special pad). The Boss 302 and Boss 429 were the only production Mustangs where the original engine block can be matched to the original car.

The Boss 429 Mustang was a limited production Mustang designed to homologate the Boss 429 engine for NASCAR racing. All were built at the Kar Kraft facility in Brighton, Michigan. Partially completed SportsRoof Mustangs that originally were to receive the 428SCJ engine were modified to accept the large 429 engine. The suspension was lowered and moved further outwards one inch, using spindles and control arms unique to the Boss 429. Other features included Boss 429 fender decals, manually controlled hood scoop, a front spoiler that was shallower than the Boss 302 spoiler, color-keyed dual racing mirrors, engine oil cooler, trunk-mounted battery, power steering, power front disc brakes, close ratio four-speed manual transmission, 3.91:1 rear axle with Traction-Lok, ¾-inch rear sway bar, chrome 15x7 Magnum 500 wheels (long center cap) with F60x15 Goodyear RWL Polyglas GT tires, the Deluxe Decor interior, 8000 rpm tachometer and AM radio.

The Boss 429 engine was based on a strengthened version of the production 429. These blocks had HP429 cast into the front of the block (driver's side). It used four-bolt mains, a forged steel crank and forged steel connecting rods. The first 279 engines were tagged 820-S and came with NASCAR-type connecting rods (with ½-inch rod bolts) while all subsequent engines were tagged 820-T and used beefed up production rods. Cylinder heads were aluminum and featured a modified hemi-type combustion chamber which Ford called "crescent." These used the "dry-deck" method, meaning no head gaskets were used. Each cylinder, oil passage and water passage had its individual "O" ring to seal it. An aluminum intake manifold with a 735 cfm Holley carburetor provided induction. The camshaft was a hydraulic type. Early engines used magnesium valve covers while later ones were aluminum.

Each Boss 429 Mustang came with a KK sticker placed on the inside of the driver's door above the Ford warranty plate which signified Kar Kraft's production number. The first Boss 429 was numbered "KK NASCAR 1201" while the last 1969 was numbered

2059. Some Boss 429s may have this silver tape stripe missing; a small brass plate was substituted by Kar Kraft on a small number of cars.

The Boss 429's serial number was stamped on the back side of the engine block assembly, on the inner front fender panels, on the transmission housing and on the chassis itself.

*1969 Boss 302*

*1969 SportsRoof GT*

# Chapter 6

# 1970 Mustang

## Production Figures

| | | | |
|---|---|---|---|
| 63A 2dr Fastback | 39,470 | 65E 2dr Hardtop | |
| 65A 2dr Hardtop | 77,161 | Grande | 13,581 |
| 76A Convertible | 6,199 | Total | 190,727 |
| 63B 2dr Fastback | 6,464 | **Specials (included in above** | |
| 65B 2dr Hardtop | 5,408 | **figures)** | |
| 76B Convertible | 1,474 | Boss 302 | 7,013 |
| 63C Fastback Mach 1 | 40,970 | Boss 429 | 499 |

## Serial Numbers

0F04F100001

0 — Last digit of model year

F — Assembly plant (F-Dearborn, R-San Jose, M-Metuchen)

04 — Plate code for Mustang (01-hardtop, 02-fastback, 03-convertible, 04-Grande, 05-Mach 1)

F — Engine code

100001 — Consecutive unit number

### Location

Stamped on plate riveted to instrument panel on driver's side, visible through the windshield; a vehicle certification label, mounted on the rear face of the driver's door, replaced the previous warranty plate.

### Engine Codes

T — 200 ci 1V 6 cyl 120 hp

L — 250 ci 1V 6 cyl 155 hp

F — 302 ci 2V V-8 220 hp

G — 302 ci 4V V-8 290 hp (Boss)

H — 351 ci 2V V-8 250 hp (351W & 351C)

M — 351 ci 4V V-8 300 hp

Q — 428 ci 4V V-8 335 hp (CJ)

R — 428 ci 4V V-8 335 hp (CJ-R)

Z — 429 ci 4V V-8 375 hp (Boss)

## V-8 Distributors

302 ci 220 hp — D0AF-12127-T

302 ci 290 hp — C9ZF-12127-E

351 ci 250 hp — D0AF-12127-H/manual, D0AF-12127-AO/automatic

351 ci 300 hp — D0OF-12127-V/manual, D0OF-12127-Z/automatic

428 ci 335 hp — D0ZF-12127-C/manual, D0ZF-12127-G/automatic

429 ci 375 hp — C9ZF-12127-D

## V-8 Carburetors

302 ci 220 hp — D0AE-9510-C/manual, D0AE-9510-D or V/automatic

302 ci 290 hp — D0ZF-9510-Z (Holley R-4653)

351 ci 250 hp — D0OF-9510-F/manual, D0OF-9510-L/automatic

351 ci 300 hp — D0OF-9510-AB/manual, D0OF-9510-AC/automatic

428 ci 335 hp — D0ZF-9510-AA or AD/manual(Holley R-4513, R-4515 [with A/C]), D0ZF-9510-AB or AC/automatic(Holley R-4514, R-4516 [with A/C])

429 ci 375 hp — D0OF-9510-S(Holley R-4647)

## Steering Gear Ratios

SMB-D — 19.9:1

SMB-F — 16.1:1

SMB-K — 16.1:1

## 1970 Mustang Prices

| | Retail |
|---|---|
| Hardtop, 65A | $2,721.00 |
| SportsRoof, 63A | 2,771.00 |
| Convertible, 76A | 3,025.00 |
| Grande, 65E | 2,926.00 |
| Mach 1, 63C | 3,271.00 |
| Boss 302 | 3,720.00 |
| 250 CID 155 hp 6 cyl extra charge over 200 CID 6 cyl | 39.00 |
| 302 CID 220 hp V-8 extra charge over 200 CID 6 cyl | 101.00 |
| 351 CID 250 hp V-8 extra charge over 302 CID V-8 | 45.00 |
| 351 CID 300 hp V-8 extra charge over 302 CID V-8 | 93.00 |
| Mach 1 over 351 CID 250 hp | 48.00 |
| 428 CID 335 hp Cobra V8 extra charge over 302 CID V-8 | 356.00 |
| Mach 1 over 351 CID 250 hp | 311.00 |
| 428 CID 335 hp Cobra Jet Ram Air (except Mach 1) | 421.00 |
| Mach 1 over 351 CID 250 hp | 376.00 |
| Boss 429 CID 4V V-8 | 1,208.00 |
| SelectShift Cruise-O-Matic (except 428) | 201.00 |
| with 428 V-8s | 222.00 |
| 4-speed manual transmission, 302, 351, 428 V-8s | 205.00 |
| Power front disc brakes (NA 200 CID 6 cyl) | 65.00 |
| Power steering | 95.00 |
| SelectAire air conditioner (NA w/200 CID, Boss 302 428 CID w/4-speed manual) | 380.00 |
| Electric clock, rectangular (NA Grande, Mach 1 or Decor Group) | 16.00 |
| Electric clock, round, Decor Group only (std. Grande, Mach 1) | 16.00 |
| Console | 54.00 |
| Convenience Group, Grande, Mach 1, Boss 302 & Decor Group | 32.00 |
| All others | 45.00 |
| Rear window defogger, 2dr Hardtops | 26.00 |
| Color-keyed dual racing mirrors | 26.00 |
| Deluxe seatbelts with reminder light | 15.00 |

| | |
|---|---:|
| Rear Sport Deck seat (SportsRoof) | 97.00 |
| Rim Blow Deluxe steering wheel | 39.00 |
| Tilt steering wheel | 45.00 |
| Intermittent windshield wipers | 26.00 |
| Space-saver spare (std. Boss 302, NA 200 CID 6 cyl) | |
|    w/E70 or F70x14 WSW or RWL tires | 7.00 |
|    w/E78x14 WSW tires | 13.00 |
|    w/E78x14 BSW tires | 20.00 |
| AM radio | 61.00 |
| AM/FM radio | 214.00 |
| Stereosonic tape (AM radio required) | 134.00 |
| Front bumper guards | 13.00 |
| Decor Group, Boss 302 and other models | 78.00 |
|   Convertibles | 97.00 |
| Rocker panel molding (std. Decor Group, NA Grande, | |
|   Mach 1 or Boss 302) | 16.00 |
| Dual accent paint stripes, Mach 1 | 13.00 |
| Vinyl roof (hardtop & Grande) | 26.00 |
| Sport Slats (requires dual racing mirrors) | 65.00 |
| Trim rings/hubcaps (std. Boss 302) | 26.00 |
| Wheel covers (std. Grande) | 26.00 |
| Sports wheel covers, Grande, Boss 302 | 32.00 |
|   All others | 58.00 |
| Wire wheel covers, Grande | 53.00 |
|   All others | 79.00 |
| Magnum 500 chrome wheels, Boss 302 only | 129.00 |
| Argent style steel wheels, Grande (NC Mach 1) | 32.00 |
|   All others | 58.00 |
| Drag Pack axle, 428 CID w/3.91 & 4.30 ratios | 155.00 |
| Optional ratio axle | 13.00 |
| Traction-Lok differential axle | 43.00 |
| Heavy-duty 55 amp battery | 13.00 |
| Heavy-duty 70 amp battery | 13.00 |
| Extra cooling package | 13.00 |
| Shaker hood scoop, Boss 302, 351 | 65.00 |
| Rear deck spoiler, SportsRoof models only | 20.00 |
| Quick ratio steering (std. Boss 302) | 16.00 |
| Competition Suspension (NA 6 cyl) | 31.00 |
| Tachometer and trip odometer (NA 6 cyl) | 54.00 |

## 1970 Exterior Colors

| Colors | Code | Colors | Code |
|---|---|---|---|
| Raven Black | A | Medium Blue Metallic | Q |
| Dark Ivy Green Metallic | C | Medium Gold Metallic | S |
| Yellow | D | Red | T |
| Medium Lime Metallic | G | Grabber Orange | U |
| Grabber Blue | J | Grabber Green | Z |
| Bright Gold Metallic | K | Calypso Coral | 1 |
| Wimbledon White | M | Light Ivy Yellow | 2 |
| Pastel Blue | N | Silver Blue Metallic | 6 |

| 1970 Interior Trim | Code | 1970 Interior Trim | Code |
|---|---|---|---|
| Black vinyl | BA | Ginger Blazer Stripe cloth | CF |
| Blue vinyl | BB | Black Houndstooth cloth & vinyl | AA |
| Vermillion vinyl | BE | Blue Houndstooth cloth & vinyl | AB |
| Ginger vinyl | BF | Vermillion Houndstooth cloth & vinyl | AE |
| Ivy vinyl | BG | Ginger Houndstooth cloth & vinyl | AF |
| White vinyl | BW | Ivy Houndstooth cloth & vinyl | AG |
| Black comfortweave vinyl | EA | Black Mach 1 knitted vinyl | 3A |
| Blue comfortweave vinyl | EB | Blue Mach 1 knitted vinyl | 3B |
| Ivy comfortweave vinyl | EG | Ivy Mach 1 knitted vinyl | 3G |
| White comfortweave vinyl | EW | White Mach 1 knitted vinyl | 3W |
| Black comfortweave vinyl | TA | Vermillion Mach 1 knitted vinyl | 3E |
| Blue comfortweave vinyl | TB | Ginger Mach 1 knitted vinyl | 3F |
| Ivy comfortweave vinyl | TG | | |
| White comfortweave vinyl | TW | | |
| Vermillion Blazer Stripe cloth | UE | | |
| Ginger Blazer Stripe cloth | UF | | |
| Vermillion Blazer Stripe cloth | CE | | |

## Convertible Top Colors

Black or White

## 1970 Mustang Facts

1970 Mustangs were mildly restyled. Headlight configuration reverted to a single seven-inch lamp on each side, this time inside the grille opening. Simulated scoops took the place of the outside headlights. The rear taillight panel was flat rather than concave and the taillights are recessed.

In the interior, a new steering wheel was used. The ignition switch was relocated on the steering column, as with all other domestic makes. The only optional interior was the Decor Group. It consisted of knitted vinyl or Blazer Stripe high-back buckets, simulated woodgrain appliques on the dash, deluxe steering wheel, molded door panels with simulated woodgrain appliques, dual color-keyed racing mirrors, and rocker panel and wheel lip moldings.

High-back bucket seats were standard equipment on all Mustangs. The Sport Slats and rear deck wing were optional on all Mustang SportsRoofs.

The Shaker scoop was again optional on engines other than the 428 CJ-R. It was available with both 351s and also on the Boss 302.

The Competition Suspension was unchanged, except for the addition of a rear stabilizer bar, ½ inch on 351s and ⅝ inch on 428 engines.

The Drag Pack option, available only with 428 engines, came with 3.91:1 or 4.30:1 axle ratios. It consisted of an engine oil cooler, stronger 427-type connecting rods and different harmonic balancer/flywheel combinations. This option changes a Cobra Jet to a Super Cobra Jet.

All 1970 Mustangs with dual exhaust systems benefited from a new exhaust system that used two mufflers mounted ahead of the rear axle, replacing the transverse muffler of previous years. All four-speed equipped Mustangs used a Hurst shifter.

While the 390 was dropped, a new 351 joined the line-up. The 351 Cleveland or 351C, available in two-barrel and four-barrel forms (250 and 300 hp) used cylinder heads which were very similar to those used on the Boss 302. The two-barrel engines used the so-called two-barrel heads which have smaller ports and valves. The four-barrel heads have the same size valves and ports as the Boss 302 cylinder heads. The 351W 4V was dropped but Mustangs equipped with the two-barrel 351 could either be a 351W or a 351C.

The Mach 1 was restyled, getting a revised grille that had two driving lamps. The NASCAR hood pins were replaced with twist-type latches and the blacked-out hood treatment of 1969 was replaced by a stripe arrangement in the middle of the hood, painted white or black. A complementary stripe was used on the rear deck lid, while the rear taillight panel got a honeycomb treatment. On the sides, aluminum rocker panel moldings with large Mach 1 lettering replaced the previous year's side tape stripes. Oval exhaust extensions replaced the quad arrangement on Mach 1s (and other Mustangs) with dual exhausts. Simulated sports wheel covers replaced the chrome styled steel wheels, but painted styled steel wheels were a no-cost option.

The Grande, too, was relatively unchanged. A half vinyl roof became part of the Grande package while in the interior, hound's-tooth cloth was used on the seats. The wire wheel covers became optional on the 1970 Grande.

The Boss 302 got a new tape stripe treatment that began on the hood (similar to the Mach 1), but then continued along the rear of the hood, down the front fenders and across the sides to the rear. Standard wheel size remained at 15x7; however, a trim ring/hubcap arrangement took the place of the Magnum 500s. Chrome Magnum 500 wheels, though, were optional but only on the Boss 302. The Shaker scoop was optional on the Boss 302.

Mechanically, the Boss 302 benefited from the redesigned dual exhaust system, the standard Hurst shifter, and the Competition Suspension which used a rear stabilizer bar measuring ⅝ inch. The engine got smaller intake valves, 2.19 inches versus 2.23 inches for 1969, which resulted in slightly better response. Aluminum valve covers replaced the chrome steel ones of 1969.

The 1970 Boss 429 featured a gloss black hood scoop, chrome Magnum 500 wheels that used a Boss 302 type center cap, the revised exhaust system and the Hurst shifter. Color availability was

Grabber Blue, Grabber Orange, Grabber Green, Calypso Coral and Pastel Blue. Interior color selection was limited to black or white.

The 1970 Boss 429 engine was the 820-T version; however, it was fitted with a mechanical lifter camshaft and a more efficient radiator fan. Some engines were tagged 820-A. These were 820-T engines that had some minor emission system modifications. The ¾ inch rear stabilizer bar was replaced by the ⅝ inch unit found on other Competition Suspension-equipped Mustangs.

A total of 499 1970 Boss 429s were built. KK numbers range from KK2060 to KK2558.

As with 1969 Bosses, all 1970 Boss 302 Mustangs had the consecutive unit number on the engine block for additional identification. The Boss 429s had additional VIN numbers on the engine block, transmission and inner fenders.

*1970 Boss 429*

# Chapter 7

# 1971 Mustang

## Production Figures

| | | |
|---|---|---|
| 65D 2dr Hardtop | 65,696 | |
| 63D 2dr SportsRoof | 23,956 | |
| 76D Convertible | 6,121 | |
| 65F 2dr Hardtop Grande | 17,406 | |
| 63F 2dr SportsRoof Mach 1 | 36,499 | |
| Total | 149,678 | |

**Specials (included in above figures)**

Boss 351      1,806

## Serial Numbers

1F01M100001

1 — Last digit of model year

F — Assembly plant (F-Dearborn, T-Metuchen)

01 — Plate code for Mustang body (01-2dr hardtop, 02-2dr SportsRoof, 03-convertible, 04-2dr hardtop Grande, 05-2dr SportsRoof Mach 1)

M — Engine code

100001 — Consecutive unit number

### Location

Stamped on plate attached to driver's side of instrument panel, visible through the windshield; certification label is attached to rear face of driver's door.

## Engine Codes

L — 250 ci 1V 6 cyl 145 hp
F — 302 ci 2V V-8 210 hp
H — 351 ci 2V V-8 240 hp
M — 351 ci 4V V-8 280 hp (CJ)

## Engine Codes

M — 351 ci 4V V-8 285 hp
R — 351 ci 4V V-8 330 hp (Boss)
C — 429 ci 4V V-8 370 hp (CJ)
J — 429 ci 4V V-8 375 hp (CJ-R)

## V-8 Distributors

302 ci 210 hp — D0AF-12127-Y/manual, D0OF-12127-AC/automatic

351 ci 240 hp — D0OF-12127-T/manual, D0OF-12127-U/automatic

351 ci 285 hp — D0OF-12127-V/manual, D0OF-12127-G/automatic

351 ci 330 hp — D0OF-12127-V(70F118)D-12

429 ci 370 hp — D0OF-12127-AA/manual, D0OF-12127-NA/automatic

429 ci 375 hp — D0OF-12127-AA(70F56)D-12/manual
D0OF-12127-NA(71F117)D-12/automatic

## V-8 Carburetors

302 ci 210 hp — D1AF-9510-BA, DA or D1OF-9510-ABA/manual, D1AF-9510-DA, AA, SA, TA or D1OF-9510-ABA/automatic

351 ci 240 hp — D1OF-9510-PA, RA, YA, ZA, D, MF, KA or
D1ZF-9510-SA, UA/manual D1MF-9510-KA, D1OF-9510-RA,
YA, ZA or D1ZF-9510-SA, UA/automatic
351 ci 280 hp — D1ZF-9510-ZA/all
351 ci 285 hp — D1OF-9510-EA/manual, D1OF-9510-AAA,
FA/automatic
351 ci 330 hp — D1ZF-9510-FA or D0ZF-9510-Z
429 ci 370 hp — D0OF-9510-A/manual, D0OF-9510-B/
automatic
429 ci 375 hp — D1OF-9510-SA or D1ZF-9510-YA(Holley
R-6127)/manual, D1OF-9510-TA or D1ZZ-9510-XA(Holley
R-6128)/automatic

## 1971 Mustang Prices — Retail

| | Retail |
|---|---|
| 2dr Hardtop | $2,911.00 |
| 2dr SportsRoof | 2,973.00 |
| Convertible | 3,227.00 |
| 2dr Hardtop Grande | 3,117.00 |
| 2dr SportsRoof Mach 1 | 3,268.00 |
| 2dr SportsRoof Boss 351 | 4,124.00 |
| 302 2V 210 hp | N/C |
| 351 2V 240 hp | 45.00 |
| 351 4V 285 hp | 93.00 |
| 429 4V 370 hp* | 372.00 |
| 429 4V 370 hp Ram Air* | 436.00 |
| Optional axle ratio (NA Boss 351) | 13.00 |
| Heavy-duty 70 ampere battery | 16.00 |
| Traction-Lok differential (std. Boss 351) | 45.00 |
| Drag Pack, 429s only 3.91 & 4.30 w/Traction-Lok | 155.00 |
| 4.30 w/No-Spin Detroit Locker | 207.00 |
| Extra cooling package | 14.00 |
| Instrumentation Group Mach 1 w/console | 37.00 |
| Mach 1 w/o console | 54.00 |
| Grande w/o console | 62.00 |
| All others | 79.00 |
| Dual Ram Air Induction (NA 250 & 302 engines) | 65.00 |
| Competition Suspension | 31.00 |
| Rear deck spoiler (SportsRoof only) | 32.00 |
| 4-speed manual, V-8 engines | 216.00 |
| SelectShift Automatic, 250, 302 & 351 engines | 217.00 |
| with 429 engine | 238.00 |
| Power front disc brakes | 70.00 |
| Power steering | 115.00 |
| Power windows | 127.00 |
| AM radio | 66.00 |
| AM/FM stereo radio | 214.00 |
| AM/stereo tape system (requires AM radio) | 134.00 |
| SelectAire air conditioner | 412.00 |
| Front & rear bumper guards (NA Mach 1) | 31.00 |
| Console (includes clock), Grande & Mach 1 | 60.00 |
| All others | 76.00 |
| Protection Group, models w/bumper guards | 34.00 |

| | |
|---|---:|
| All others | 45.00 |
| Sport Deck seat | 97.00 |
| Rim Blow steering wheel | 39.00 |
| Tilt-away steering wheel (requires power steering) | 45.00 |
| Trim, Decor Group, Convertible & Boss 351 | 97.00 |
| All others | 78.00 |
| Sports Interior, Mach 1 & SportsRoof | 130.00 |
| Boss 351 | 88.00 |
| Bodyside tape stripe (Mach 1 only, std. Boss 351) | 26.00 |
| Vinyl roof, 2dr Hardtop (std. Grande) | 89.00 |
| Base wheel covers | 26.00 |
| Sport wheel covers, Grande | 32.00 |
| Mach 1 | 23.00 |
| All others | 58.00 |
| Trim rings/hubcaps, Grande | 9.00 |
| All others | 35.00 |
| Magnum 500 chrome wheels (requires Competition Suspension, F60x15 RWL tires, & includes | |
| Space-saver spare), Grande | 129.00 |
| Boss 351 & Mach 1 | 120.00 |
| All others | 155.00 |
| Intermittent windshield wipers | 26.00 |
| Rear window electric defroster | 48.00 |
| Color-keyed dual racing mirrors | 26.00 |
| Deluxe seatbelts | 17.00 |
| Complete tinted glass, Convertible | 15.00 |
| All others | 40.00 |
| Convenience Group | 51.00 |
| Tires | |
| E78x14 WSW | 32.00 |
| E70x14 Wide Oval WSW over E78x14 | 39.00 |
| F70x14 Wide Oval WSW over E78x14 | 68.00 |
| F60x15 Wide Oval BSW/WL over E78x14 | 99.00 |
| F70x14 Wide Oval BSW/WL over E70x14 WSW | 81.00 |
| F70x14 Wide Oval WSW over E70x14 WSW | 29.00 |
| F70x14 Wide Oval BSW/WL over E70x14 WSW | 42.00 |
| F60x15 Wide Oval BSW/WL over E70x14 WSW | 60.00 |
| F70x14 Wide Oval BSW/WL over F70x14 WSW | 13.00 |
| F60x15 Wide Oval BSW/WL over F70x14 WSW | 31.00 |
| F60x15 Wide Oval BSW/WL over F70x14 BSW/WL | 18.00 |

*Includes 80 amp heavy-duty battery, Competition Suspension, 55 amp alternator, extra cooling package, dual exhausts, bright engine dress-up with cast aluminum rocker covers, Mach 1 hood, plus a 3.50 non-locking axle with Ram Air and a 3.25 non-locking axle with non-Ram Air. Requires optional transmission, & Drag Pack when 3.91 or 4.30 axle is ordered plus Ram Air: F70x14 Wide Oval belted WSW tires, F70x14 BSW/WL on Mach 1. non-Ram Air: E70x14 Wide Oval belted WSW tires, except Mach 1 Air conditioner not available with Drag Pack and Ram Air.

## 1971 Exterior Colors

| Colors | Code |
|---|---|
| Raven Black | A |
| Maroon Metallic | B |
| Dark Ivy Green Metallic | C |
| Grabber Yellow | D |
| Medium Yellow Gold | E |
| Grabber Lime | I |
| Grabber Blue | J |
| Wimbledon White | M |
| Pastel Blue | N |
| Medium Green Metallic | P |
| Light Pewter Metallic | V |
| Grabber Green Metallic | Z |
| Bright Red | 3 |
| Medium Brown Metallic | 5 |
| Silver Blue Metallic | 6 |
| Light Gold | 8 |
| Gold Metallic | Special |
| Gold Glamour | Special |

## 1971 Interior Trim

| Trim | Code |
|---|---|
| Black vinyl | 1A |
| Medium Blue vinyl | 1B |
| Vermillion vinyl | 1E |
| Medium Ginger vinyl | 1F |
| Medium Green vinyl | 1R |
| White vinyl | 1W |
| Black knitted vinyl | 3A |
| White knitted vinyl | 3W |
| Vermillion cloth & vinyl | 2E |
| Medium Ginger cloth & vinyl | 2F |
| Medium Blue cloth & vinyl | 2B |
| Medium Green cloth & vinyl | 2R |
| Black knitted vinyl | 5A |
| White knitted vinyl | 5W |
| Vermillion knitted vinyl | 5E |
| Medium Blue knitted vinyl | 5B |
| Medium Green knitted vinyl | 5R |
| Medium Ginger knitted vinyl | 5F |
| Black knitted vinyl | CA |
| White knitted vinyl | CW |
| Vermillion knitted vinyl | CE |
| Medium Blue knitted vinyl | CB |
| Medium Green knitted vinyl | CR |
| Medium Ginger knitted vinyl | CF |
| Black cloth & vinyl | 4A |
| Medium Blue cloth & vinyl | 4B |
| Vermillion cloth & vinyl | 4E |
| Medium Ginger cloth & vinyl | 4F |
| Medium Green cloth & vinyl | 4R |

## 1971 Mustang Facts

While maintaining a basic resemblance to previous Mustangs, the 1971 Mustangs were the largest and heaviest yet. Every dimension increased; Wheelbase was stretched to 109 inches.

Engine choice still remained high; a total of ten different engines were available on the Mustang.

Base engine was the 250 ci six-cylinder on all models except the Mach 1 which came with the 210 hp 302 and the Boss 351 which got a 330 hp version of the 351.

Optional V-8s were the 210 hp 302, 240 hp 351, 285 hp 351, 370 hp 429 and 375 hp 429. All 351 V-8s were 351Cs. In May 1971, a low-compression 351CJ replaced the 285 hp 351 that was available at the beginning of the model year, rated at 280 hp. Both of these 351s had the same engine code, M.

The 428CJ was replaced by the 429CJ as the top Mustang engine option. The 429 belonged to the 385 Engine Series and as such, no parts were interchangeable with the 428. Wider, larger and heavier, the 429 would not readily fit into the 1970 Mustang engine compartment, which is one of the reasons that the 1971 Mustang got bigger. The bottom end and cylinder block were a variation of the 429/460 block, on which the Boss 429 was also based. The cylinder heads were similar to the 351 Cleveland in design. You could describe the 429 as a large Boss 302. As equipped in the Mustang, the 429CJ came with four-bolt mains, forged rods and pistons, 11.3:1 compression ratio, a hydraulic cam (similar to the Boss 429's), very large ports and valves, 2.25 inch intake and 1.72 inch exhausts. Regular production 429/460 engines came with cylinder heads that had smaller ports and valves. The 429CJ came with a Rochester Quadrajet four-barrel carburetor, and some early units had adjustable valve trains. All 429CJs came with aluminum valve covers.

The 429CJ became a 429SCJ if the Drag Pack option was ordered. It consisted of a 3.91:1 or 4.30:1 rear axle ratio with Traction-Lok or a 4.11:1 ratio with a Detroit Locker rear. Both of these engines had the engine code C. Some Mustangs with the Drag Pack also included an external engine oil cooler, though of a different design than previously used. The SCJ engine came with a 780 cfm carburetor rather than the Rochester Quadrajet, a mechanical lifter camshaft and adjustable rocker arms.

Mustangs equipped with the 429CJ Ram Air engine got the letter J for the engine code in the VIN. It was rated at 375 hp. The 429CJ-R engine could either be a CJ or SCJ, if it had the Drag Pack option or not.

All four-speed manual transmissions came with a Hurst shifter.

The Competition Suspension, available only on Mustangs with 351-2V engines and larger, consisted of heavier-duty shock absorbers, springs and front and rear stabilizer bars (rear bars for 351 four-barrel and larger engines only), and staggered rear shocks (except for the 351-2V engine). Mustangs with this option got power steering with variable ratio. The Competition Suspension was also mandatory with the optional 15x7 chrome Magnum 500 wheels.

The Dual Ram Induction option consisted of a hood with two functional NASA-type hood scoops, which were controlled by engine vacuum. Twist-type hood locks, a Tu-tone paint treatment, black or argent, and Ram Air decals rounded out the option. It was available only on 351 and larger engines.

The optional variable ratio steering had a 15.7:1 ratio.

While the rear deck spoiler remained on the option list, the Sport Slats were deleted, due to the low angle of the SportsRoof's rear window.

For the first time, power windows and an electric rear window defroster were optional. The electric defroster was not available on convertibles.

The four-pod instrument panel of 1969-70 was replaced by a three-pod design. Two large pods with a smaller one in between them dominated the driver's side of the dash. The large left pod consisted of four warning lights: oil pressure, temperature, brakes and alternator. The center pod was for fuel while the large right unit housed the speedometer.

The optional instrumentation group (standard on the Boss 351 and not available with the 250 ci six-cylinder) consisted of three instruments, oil pressure, alternator and temperature, housed in a panel located above the radio. The warning lights on the left large pod were displaced by an 8000 rpm tachometer.

The three-spoke Rim Blow steering wheel was optional. Similar to the one used on 1969-70 Mustangs, it used a redesigned center pad. The tilt steering is optional; however, power steering was a mandatory option.

The Decor Group (not available on the Mach 1 or Grande) consisted of either knitted vinyl or cloth inserts for the seats, black instrument panel faces, the deluxe two-spoke steering wheel, molded door panels (available only on the convertible and Boss 351), rear ashtray, dual color-keyed racing mirrors, and rocker panel and wheel lip moldings. The moldings were not available with the Boss 351.

The Mach 1 Sports Interior, available on the Mach 1 and all other SportsRoofs, consisted of knitted vinyl seats, the two-spoke deluxe steering wheel, molded door panels, black dash panel applique, woodgrain applique for the center instrument panel, rear ashtray, electric clock, the instrumentation group, bright pedal pads, and color-keyed rubber floor mats stitched directly on the carpets (front only).

The fold-down rear seat option included a Space-saver spare tire.

The Mach 1 for 1971 used a different grille-bumper combination. The honeycomb grille housed two driving lamps while the front bumper was covered with urethane color-keyed to the Mustang's paint. Fender moldings were also color-keyed. The NASA hood was standard equipment (non-functional). The hood along with the lower body were painted either black or argent, depending on body paint. Color-keyed dual racing mirrors were standard and all Mach 1s came with front fender Mach 1 decals. There was also a small Mach 1 decal on the rear deck above the pop-open gas cap. Boss 351 side stripes were optional.

Standard engine with the Mach 1 was the 302 V-8, and all other V-8s were optional, except the 330 hp 351 found on the Boss 351.

The Boss 351 replaced the Boss 302 and the Boss 429 as the premier performance Mustang. Like previous Boss Mustangs, it was a complete package, with limited options. Standard was the 330 hp 351 Cleveland featuring a four-bolt main block, large port cylinder heads and valves, a solid lifter camshaft, an 11.7:1 compression ratio and aluminum valve covers. Other standard features were Ram Air, 3.91:1 rear axle with Traction-Lok, four-speed manual transmission, Competition Suspension, power front disc brakes, front spoiler, the Mach 1 front grille and lower body side paint treatment, bodyside tape treatment and Boss 351 decals in place of the Mach 1 decals. The Boss 351, however, came with the standard chrome front bumper. The hood differed from the Mach 1's as the black or argent paint covered most of the hood.

Standard wheels on the Boss 351 were 15x7 with trim rings/hubcaps. Optional were the 15x7 chrome Magnum 500s. Tires in both cases were Goodyear F60x15 RWL.

The Grande was still promoted as the luxury Mustang, available only on the hardtop body style. A full vinyl roof, Grande lettering on the "C" pillar, dual accent paint stripe, color-keyed racing mirrors, bright rocker panel and wheel lip moldings, and special Grande wheel covers were all standard equipment on the exterior. In the interior, the Grande came with the Deluxe two-spoke steering wheel, black dash panel appliques, woodgrain appliques in the center dash, molded door panels, Lambeth cloth seat inserts, electric clock, rear ashtray and bright trim on the pedals. All Mustang engines were available on the Grande.

Further watering down the overall performance image of the Mach 1 and Boss 351 Mustangs was the availability of the Sports Hardtop option late in the model year. Based on the hardtop body, it used the Mach 1's honeycomb grille and color-keyed bumper, the standard Mach 1 hubcap/trim rings, the non-functional NASA hood and the Boss 351's side stripes.

*1971 Mach 1*

*1971 Boss 351*

# Chapter 8

# 1972 Mustang

## Production Figures

| | | | |
|---|---|---|---|
| 65D 2dr Hardtop | 57,350 | 63R 2dr SportsRoof | |
| 63D 2dr SportsRoof | 15,622 | Mach 1 | 27,675 |
| 76C Convertible | 6,121 | Total | 125,093 |
| 65F 2dr Hardtop | | | |
| Grande | 18,045 | | |

## Serial Numbers

2F05Q100001

2 — Last digit of model year

F — Assembly plant (F-Dearborn)

05 — Plate code for Mustang (01-2dr hardtop, 02-2dr SportsRoof, 03-convertible, 04-2dr hardtop Grande, 05-2dr SportsRoof Mach 1)

Q — Engine code

100001 — Consecutive unit number

**Location**

Stamped on plate riveted to driver's side of dash, visible through the windshield; certification label attached to rear face of driver's door.

**Engine Codes**

L — 250 ci 1V 6 cyl 98 hp

F — 302 ci 2V V-8 140 hp

H — 351 ci 2V V-8 177 hp

Q — 351 ci 4V V-8 266 hp (CJ)

R — 351 ci 4V V-8 275 hp (HO)

## 1972 Mustang Prices                    Retail

| | |
|---|---|
| 6 cyl Models | |
| 2dr Hardtop, 65D | $2,679.00 |
| 2dr SportsRoof, 63D | 2,736.00 |
| 2dr Convertible, 76D | 2,965.00 |
| Grande Hardtop, 65F | 2,865.00 |
| 8 cyl Models | |
| 2dr Hardtop, 65D | 2,766.00 |
| 2dr SportsRoof, 63D | 2,823.00 |
| 2dr Convertible, 76D | 3,051.00 |
| Grande Hardtop, 65F | 2,952.00 |
| Mach 1 SportsRoof, 63R | 3,003.00 |
| 351 cid 2V 8 cyl | 40.79 |
| 351 cid 4V 8 cyl (includes NASA hood) | 115.44 |
| 351 cid 4V HO 8 cyl, with Mach 1 | 783.00 |
| All others | 812.00 |
| SelectShift Cruise-O-Matic transmission | 203.73 |
| 4-speed manual with Hurst shifter | 192.99 |
| SelectAire air conditioner | 367.59 |

| | |
|---|---|
| Axle, optional ratio | 11.66 |
| Axle, Traction-Lok differential | 42.64 |
| Battery, heavy-duty 70 ampere | 13.52 |
| Belts, deluxe | 15.49 |
| Bumper guards, front & rear | 28.19 |
| Console, Grande & Mach 1 Sports Interior | 53.40 |
| all others | 67.95 |
| Convenience group | 45.53 |
| Decor group | 69.79 |
| Door edge guards | 5.78 |
| Electric defroster, rear window | 42.64 |
| Emission system, Calif. | 13.87 |
| Extra cooling package | 12.59 |
| Complete tinted glass, Convertible | 13.52 |
| All other models | 35.94 |
| Hood, NASA-type (std. Mach 1 with 351) | N/C |
| Instrumentation Group, Grande without console | 55.24 |
| All others | 70.83 |
| Mirrors, outside color-keyed dual racing | 23.23 |
| Paint, color-glow | 34.90 |
| Power front disc brakes | 62.05 |
| Power side windows | 113.48 |
| Power steering | 102.85 |
| Protection package | 52.06 |
| Radio, AM | 59.17 |
| Radio, AM/FM stereo | 191.01 |
| Ram Induction NASA hood (with 351 2V only) | 58.24 |
| Roof, vinyl | 79.51 |
| Roof, ¾ vinyl | 52.35 |
| Seat, Sport Deck rear | 86.32 |
| Spoiler, rear deck (SportsRoof models only) | 29.12 |
| Sports Interior option, Mach 1 | 115.44 |
| Steering wheel, Rim Blow, Deluxe three–spoke | 34.90 |
| Steering wheel, tilt | 40.79 |
| Stereosonic tape system | 120.29 |
| Suspension, competition | 28.19 |
| Tape stripe, black or argent bodyside | 23.23 |
| Trim rings/hubcaps, Grande | 7.86 |
| All others | 31.08 |
| Wheel covers | 23.23 |
| Wheel covers, Sports, Grande | 56.18 |
| Mach 1 & Decor Group | 48.33 |
| All others | 79.40 |
| Wheels, Magnum 500 Chrome, Grande | 115.44 |
| Mach 1 & Decor Group | 107.59 |
| All others | 138.67 |
| Windshield wipers, intermittent | 23.23 |
| Glass, tinted windshield | 22.42 |
| Models having (5) E78x14 BSW tires, extra charge for: | |
| (5) E70x14 WSW | 35.28 |
| (5) F70x14 WSW | 61.78 |
| (5) F70x14 B/WL | 73.57 |

|  |  |
|---|---|
| (4) F60x15 B/WL (includes F78x14 Space-saver spare) | 90.96 |

Models having (5) E70x14 WSW tires, extra charge for:

|  |  |
|---|---|
| (5) F70x14 WSW | 26.51 |
| (5) F70x14 B/WL | 38.36 |
| (4) F60x15 B/WL (includes F78x14 Space-saver spare) | 55.68 |

## 1972 Exterior Colors

| Colors | Code |
|---|---|
| Wimbledon White | 9A |
| Bright Red | 2B |
| Medium Yellow Gold | 6C |
| Bright Lime | 4E |
| Grabber Blue | 3F |
| Medium Brown Metallic | 5H |
| Bright Blue Metallic | 3J |
| Medium Green Metallic | 4P |
| Dark Green Metallic | 4Q |
| Maroon | 2J |
| Light Blue | 3B |
| Medium Lime Metallic | 4F |
| Light Pewter Metallic | 5A |
| Medium Bright Yellow | 6E |
| Gold Glow | 6F |
| Ivy Glow | 4C |

## 1972 Interior Trim

| Trim | Code |
|---|---|
| Medium Ginger cloth & vinyl | 4F |
| Vermillion cloth & vinyl | 4E |
| Medium Blue cloth & vinyl | 4B |
| Medium Green cloth & vinyl | 4R |
| Black cloth & vinyl | 4A |
| Medium Blue knitted vinyl | 5B |
| Black knitted vinyl | 5A |

## 1972 Interior Trim

| Trim | Code |
|---|---|
| Vermillion knitted vinyl | 5E |
| White knitted vinyl | 5W |
| Medium Green knitted vinyl | 5R |
| Medium Ginger knitted vinyl | 5F |
| Vermillion vinyl | 1E |
| White vinyl | 1W |
| Black vinyl | 1A |
| Medium Blue vinyl | 1B |
| Medium Green vinyl | 1R |
| Medium Ginger vinyl | 1F |
| Vermillion cloth & vinyl | 2E |
| Medium Ginger cloth & vinyl | 2F |
| Medium Blue cloth & vinyl | 2B |
| Medium Green cloth & vinyl | 2R |
| Black knitted vinyl | CA |
| White knitted vinyl | CW |
| Vermillion knitted vinyl | CE |
| Medium Blue knitted vinyl | CB |
| Medium Green knitted vinyl | CR |
| Medium Ginger knitted vinyl | CF |

## Convertible Top Colors

Black or White

## 1972 Mustang Facts

The 1972 Mustangs were externally similar to the '71s. You could tell them apart by the Mustang script lettering on the deck lid above the right taillights—1971 Mustangs had Mustang lettering that covered the width of the deck lid. All Mustangs came with chrome rocker panel and wheel lip moldings except for the Mach 1. These were previously optional.

The Exterior Decor Group, available only on the standard hardtops and convertibles, gave these Mustang models more of a performance look. It consisted of the Mach 1 honeycomb grille and sportslamps, color-keyed front bumper, hood and fender moldings, lower bodyside paint treatment and the trim ring/hubcap arrangement for the wheels. The Exterior Decor Group could be combined with the Mach 1 tape bodyside stripes to give Mustangs so equipped the look of performance.

The base engine was the 250 ci six-cylinder. The standard Mach 1 engine was still the 302 ci V-8. Optional were two 351s, a 2V version rated at 177 hp and the 4V 351CJ rated at 266 hp.

The 351 HO was available for a brief time on all 1972 Mustang body styles. As such, it represented Ford's last true 1960s-style muscle engine/package. The 351 HO was essentially a low compression Boss 351 engine, pumping out 275 hp. About 1,000 or so of these engines were installed in Mustangs and they all came with a four-speed manual transmission, 3.91 Traction-Lok rear axle, dual exhausts, Competition Suspension, power front disc brakes and an electronic rev limiter. Tires were F60x15 on the chrome Magnum 500 wheels. No special identification was used other than a 351 HO decal on the air cleaner lid.

Two special Mustang Sprint packages were made available on Mustang SportsRoof and hardtop models in February 1972, to coincide with similar Pintos and Mavericks. Sprint Package A consisted of the Exterior Decor Group, dual color-keyed racing mirrors, trim rings/hubcap combination with E70x14 WSW tires. What made the Sprints stand out were their white paint with dual blue and red hood stripes, blue and red lower body treatment and a blue and red rear taillight panel. A USA shield was used on the rear fenders while the interior, too, was unique with white vinyl interior. Seats were white vinyl with blue Lambeth cloth.

Sprint Package B was identical but added the Competition Suspension and the chrome Magnum 500 wheels/F60x15 tire combination.

Fifty Sprint Package A convertibles were built for the Washington D.C. area for participation in the Cherry Day Parade.

*1972 SportsRoof Sprint*

# Chapter 9

# 1973 Mustang

## Production Figures

| | | | |
|---|---|---|---|
| 63D 2dr SportsRoof | 10,820 | 63R 2dr SportsRoof | |
| 65D 2dr Hardtop | 51,480 | Mach 1 | 35,440 |
| 76D Convertible | 11,853 | Total | 134,867 |
| 65F 2dr Hardtop | | | |
| Grande | 25,274 | | |

## Serial Numbers

3F03H100001

3 — Last digit of model year

F — Assembly plant (F-Dearborn)

03 — Plate code for Mustang (01-2dr hardtop, 02-2dr SportsRoof, 03-convertible, 04-2dr hardtop Grande, 05-2dr SportsRoof Mach 1)

H — Engine code

100001 — Consecutive unit number

### Location

Stamped on plate riveted to driver's side of dash, visible through the windshield; certification label attached to rear face of driver's door.

### Engine Codes

| | |
|---|---|
| L — 250 ci 1V 6 cyl 99 hp | H — 351 ci 2V V-8 177 hp |
| F — 302 ci 2V V-8 141 hp | Q — 351 ci 4V V-8 266 hp (CJ) |

## 1973 Mustang Prices                          Retail

| | |
|---|---|
| 6 cyl Models | |
| 2dr Hardtop, 65D | $2,760.00 |
| 2dr SportsRoof, 63D | 2,820.00 |
| 2dr Convertible, 76D | 3,102.00 |
| 2dr Hardtop, Grande, 65F | 2,946.00 |
| 8 cyl Models | |
| 2dr Hardtop, 65D | 2,847.00 |
| 2dr SportsRoof, 63D | 2,907.00 |
| 2dr Convertible, 76D | 3,189.00 |
| 2dr Hardtop, Grande, 65F | 3,033.00 |
| 2dr SportsRoof Mach 1, 63R | 3,088.00 |
| 351 cid 2V 8 cyl | 40.79 |
| 351 cid 4V 8 cyl | 107.00 |
| SelectShift Cruise-O-Matic | 203.73 |
| 4-speed manual with Hurst shifter | 192.99 |
| Air conditioner, SelectAire | 367.59 |
| Axle, optional ratio | 11.66 |

| | |
|---|---:|
| Axle, Traction-Lok differential | 42.64 |
| Battery, heavy-duty 70 ampere | 13.52 |
| Belts, Deluxe | 15.49 |
| Bumper Group, Deluxe | 25.00 |
| Bumper Guards, rear | 14.00 |
| Console, Grande | 53.40 |
| All others | 67.95 |
| Convenience Group | 45.53 |
| Decor Group | 51.00 |
| Door edge guards | 5.78 |
| Electric rear window defroster | 57.00 |
| Emissions testing, Calif. | 13.87 |
| Extra cooling package | 12.59 |
| Floor mats, front color-keyed | 13.30 |
| Complete tinted glass, Convertible | 13.52 |
| All others | 35.94 |
| Hood, NASA-type | N/C |
| Instrumentation Group, Grande without console | 55.24 |
| All others | 70.83 |
| Mirrors, outside color-keyed dual racing | 23.23 |
| Paint, Metallic Glow | 34.90 |
| Paint, Tu-tone hood (NA w/Dual Ram Induction) | |
| Mach 1 | 18.00 |
| All others | 34.00 |
| Power front disc brakes | 62.05 |
| Power side windows | 113.48 |
| Power steering | 102.85 |
| Protection Group, Grande | 23.38 |
| All others | 36.00 |
| Radio, AM | 59.17 |
| Radio, AM/FM stereo | 191.01 |
| Dual Ram Induction option (w/351 cid 2V only) | 58.24 |
| Roof, vinyl | 79.51 |
| Roof, ¾ vinyl | 52.35 |
| Seat, Sport Deck rear | 86.32 |
| Spoiler, rear deck (SportsRoof & Mach 1) | 29.12 |
| Sports Interior option, Mach 1 | 115.44 |
| Steering wheel, leather-wrapped | 23.10 |
| Steering wheel, Rim Blow, Deluxe 3–spoke | 34.90 |
| Steering wheel, tilt | 40.79 |
| Stereosonic tape system | 120.29 |
| Suspension, competition | 28.19 |
| Tape stripe, black or argent bodyside | 23.23 |
| Trim rings/hubcaps, Grande | 7.86 |
| All others | 31.08 |
| Wheel covers | 23.23 |
| Wheel covers, sports, Grande | 56.18 |
| Mach 1 & Decor Group | 48.33 |
| All others | 79.40 |
| Wheels, forged aluminum, Grande | 118.77 |
| Mach 1 & Decor Group | 110.92 |
| All others | 142.00 |

| | |
|---|---|
| Windshield wipers, interval | 23.23 |
| Glass, tinted windshield | 22.42 |

Models having (5) E78x14 BSW tires, extra charge for:

| | |
|---|---|
| (5) F78x14 BSW | 17.00 |
| (5) E70x14 WSW | 35.28 |
| (5) F70x14 WSW | 61.78 |
| (5) F70x14 B/WL | 73.57 |
| (5) GR78x14 steel-belted radial ply BSW | 115.00 |
| (5) GR78x14 steel-belted radial ply WSW | 144.00 |

Models having (5) F78x14 tires, extra charge for:

| | |
|---|---|
| (5) F70x14 WSW | 46.00 |
| (5) F70x14 B/WL | 57.00 |
| (5) GR78x14 steel-belted radial ply BSW | 98.00 |
| (5) GR78x14 steel-belted radial ply WSW | 127.00 |

Models having E70x14 WSW tires, extra charge for:

| | |
|---|---|
| (5) F70x14 WSW | 26.51 |
| (5) F70x14 B/WL | 38.36 |
| (5) GR78x14 steel-belted radial ply BSW | 69.00 |
| (5) GR78x14 steel-belted radial ply WSW | 98.00 |

## 1973 Exterior Colors

| Colors | Code |
|---|---|
| Wimbledon White | 9A |
| Bright Red | 2B |
| Medium Yellow Gold | 6C |
| Medium Blue Metallic | 3D |
| Medium Brown Metallic | 5H |
| Blue Glow | 3K |
| Medium Copper Metallic | 5M |
| Medium Aqua | 4N |
| Medium Green Metallic | 4P |
| Dark Green Metallic | 4Q |
| Saddle Bronze Metallic | 5T |
| Light Blue | 3B |
| Medium Bright Yellow | 6E |
| Ivy Glow | 4C |
| Bright Green Gold Metallic | 4B |
| Gold Glow | 6F |

## 1973 Interior Trim

| Trim | Code |
|---|---|
| Black vinyl | AA |
| Medium Blue vinyl | AB |
| Medium Ginger vinyl | AF |
| Avocado vinyl | AG |

## 1973 Interior Trim

| Trim | Code |
|---|---|
| White vinyl | AW |
| Black knitted vinyl | CA |
| Medium Blue knitted vinyl | CB |
| Medium Ginger knitted vinyl | CF |
| Avocado knitted vinyl | CG |
| White knitted vinyl | CW |
| Black cloth & vinyl | FA |
| Medium Blue cloth & vinyl | FB |
| Medium Ginger cloth & vinyl | FF |
| Avocado cloth & vinyl | FG |
| Black Mach 1 knitted vinyl | GA |
| Medium Blue Mach 1 knitted vinyl | GB |
| Medium Ginger Mach 1 knitted vinyl | GF |
| Avocado Mach 1 knitted vinyl | GG |
| White Mach 1 knitted vinyl | GW |

## Convertible Top Colors

Black or White

## 1973 Mustang Facts

1973 is significant for it was the last year of the first generation Mustangs. All three Mustang body styles were available but it was the last year for the factory-built convertible. Convertibles would become available again in 1983. 1973 Mustangs were slightly restyled to distinguish them from the 1972s, but in most respects they were unchanged.

The most noticeable change was the redesigned grille. The eggcrate mesh was larger and the turn signal lamps were located within the grille opening. Headlight location remained unchanged; however, the headlight bezel was chrome. Similarly, the taillight bezels were finished in bright metal.

The front bumper, designed to meet the new federal 5 mph standards, was color-keyed to the car's paint. The hood and fender moldings also were color-keyed.

The rear bumper, similar to the 1971–72 unit, was mounted further away from the rear of the car in order to comply with 2½ mph rear standards.

The Decor Group, similar to the 1972 option, used a blacked-out grille with a small Mustang running horse emblem in the center. As with 1972 Mustangs, the optional bodyside tape stripe in black or argent was optional with the Decor Group.

The Mach 1 got a new bodyside tape stripe treatment. A three-quarter vinyl roof was optional on the Mach 1 and all other Sports-Roof models.

The Grande was unchanged, save for colors and vinyl roof treatments.

The non-functional NASA hood was standard equipment on the Mach 1 with the 351 engines and a no-cost option with the 302 engine. The functional hood was optionally available only with the 351 2V engine.

Mustangs with the Tu-tone hood option got the non-functional NASA hood painted either low-gloss black or argent with twist-type hood locks.

Engine availability was unchanged from 1972. The Hurst shifter that came with four-speed equipped Mustangs used a round knob rather than the distinctive Hurst T handle.

*1973 convertible*

# Chapter 10

# 1974 Mustang II

## Production Figures

| | | | |
|---|---|---|---|
| 60F 2dr Hardtop | 177,671 | 69R 3dr Hatchback | |
| 69F 3dr Hatchback | 74,799 | Mach 1 | 44,046 |
| 60H 2dr Hardtop Ghia | 89,477 | Total | 385,993 |

## Serial Numbers

4R02Y100001

4 — Last digit of model year

R — Assembly plant (F-Dearborn, R-San Jose)

02 — Plate code for Mustang (02-2dr hardtop, 03-3dr hatchback, 04-2dr hardtop Ghia, 05-3dr hatchback Mach 1)

Y — Engine code

100001 — Consecutive unit number

### Location

Stamped on plate riveted to driver's dash, visible through the windshield; certification label attached to rear face of driver's door.

### Engine Codes

Y — 140 ci 2.3L 2V 4 cyl 88 hp

Z — 171 ci 2.8L 2V V-6 105 hp

## 1974 Mustang II Prices                    Retail

| | |
|---|---|
| 4 cyl Models | |
| 2dr Hardtop, 60F | $3,134.00 |
| 3dr 2+2, 69F | 3,328.00 |
| 2dr Ghia, 60H | 3,480.00 |
| 6 cyl Models | |
| 3dr Mach 1, 69R | 3,674.00 |
| Extra charge over 2.3 liter 4 cyl | |
| 2.8 liter V-6 | 229.00 |
| Credit for 2.3 liter substitution on Mach 1 | (229.00) |
| SelectShift Cruise-O-Matic | 212.00 |
| Accent Group | 151.00 |
| Air conditioner, SelectAire | 390.00 |
| Alarm system, anti-theft | 75.00 |
| Automatic seatback release | 24.00 |
| Axle, Traction-Lok differential | 45.00 |
| Battery, heavy-duty | 14.00 |
| Belts, color-keyed deluxe | 17.00 |
| Bumper guards, front and rear | 37.00 |
| Clock, digital quartz crystal | 36.00 |
| Console | 53.00 |
| Convenience Group: | |
| Models with Luxury Interior Group | 41.00 |

| | |
|---|---|
| Mach 1, models w/Rallye Package or Accent Group | 21.00 |
| Ghia, models w/Luxury Interior Group in combination with Rallye Package or Mach 1 in combination with Luxury Interior Group | 4.00 |
| All other models | 57.00 |
| Electric rear window defroster | 59.00 |
| Emission equipment, Calif. | 19.00 |
| Glass, tinted complete | 39.00 |
| Light Group | 44.00 |
| Luxury Interior Group | 100.00 |
| Maintenance Group | 44.00 |
| Mirrors, outside color-keyed remote control | 36.00 |
| Molding, rocker panel | 14.00 |
| Molding, vinyl insert bodyside | 50.00 |
| Paint, glamour | 41.00 |
| Pin stripes | 14.00 |
| Power front disc brakes | 45.00 |
| Power rack and pinion steering | 107.00 |
| Protection Group, Mach 1 | 41.00 |
| All others | 47.00 |
| Radio, AM | 61.00 |
| Radio, AM/FM monaural | 124.00 |
| Radio, AM/FM stereo | 222.00 |
| Radio with tape player, AM/FM stereo | 346.00 |
| Rallye Package (requires 2.8 V-6): | |
| Mach 1 | 150.00 |
| 3dr 2+2 | 200.00 |
| All others | 244.00 |
| Rear quarter window, flipper (3dr only) | 29.00 |
| Roof, vinyl | 83.00 |
| Seat, fold-down rear (std. 3dr) | 61.00 |
| Steering wheel, leather-wrapped | 30.00 |
| Sunroof, manually operated (2dr only) | 149.00 |
| Suspension, competition | 37.00 |
| Trim, luggage compartment | 28.00 |
| Trim, Picardy velour cloth (Ghia) | 62.00 |
| Trim rings (w/styled steel wheels) | 32.00 |
| Wheels, four forged aluminum: | |
| Mach 1, models w/Rallye package, 3dr 2+2 models w/Accent Group | 71.00 |
| 3dr 2+2 or hardtops with Accent Group | 103.00 |
| Ghia | 103.00 |
| Hardtop | 147.00 |
| Wheels, four styled steel (std. 3dr, models with Rallye Package, and base 2dr with Accent Group) | |
| Ghia | N/C |
| Hardtop | 44.00 |
| Models having (5) BR78x13 BSW steel-belted radial tires, extra charge for five: | |
| BR78x13 steel-belted radial WSW | 30.00 |
| BR70x13 Wide Oval steel-belted radial B/WL | 59.00 |
| CR70x13 Wide Oval steel-belted radial B/WL | 77.00 |

| | |
|---|---:|
| CR70x13 Wide Oval steel-belted radial WSW | 65.00 |
| Credit for five: | |
| B78x13 BSW | (84.00) |
| B78x13 WSW | (54.00) |
| Models having (5) BR78x13 WSW steel-belted radial tires, extra charge for five: | |
| BR70x13 Wide Oval steel-belted radial B/WL | 29.00 |
| CR70x13 Wide Oval steel-belted radial B/WL | 47.00 |
| CR70x13 Wide Oval steel-belted radial WSW | 34.00 |
| Models having (5) BR70x13 B/WL Wide Oval steel-belted radial tires, extra charge for five: | |
| CR70x13 Wide Oval steel-belted radial B/WL | 17.00 |
| CR70x13 Wide Oval steel-belted radial WSW | 5.00 |

## 1974 Exterior Colors

| Colors | Code |
|---|---|
| Pearl White | 9C |
| Silver Metallic | 1G |
| Bright Red | 2B |
| Dark Red | 2M |
| Light Blue | 3B |
| Medium Bright Blue Metallic | 3N |
| Bright Green Gold Metallic | 4B |
| Medium Lime Yellow | 4W |
| Medium Copper Metallic | 5M |
| Saddle Bronze Metallic | 5T |
| Medium Yellow Gold | 6C |

## 1974 Exterior Colors

| Colors | Code |
|---|---|
| Green Glow | 4T |
| Ginger Glow | 5J |
| Tan Glow | 5U |

## 1974 Interior Trim

| Trim | Code |
|---|---|
| Black | A |
| Blue | B |
| Red | D |
| Avocado | G |
| White/Tan | M |
| White/Red | N |
| Silver | P |
| White/Blue | Q |
| Tan | U |

## 1974 Mustang II Facts

The 1974 Mustang II was a total departure from previous Mustangs. Downsized, it was available only in two body styles—a two-door hardtop and a three-door hatchback. There were no convertibles. It did incorporate many of the first generation Mustang's styling cues such as the long hood/short deck configuration, the side sculpturing and the front grille.

Mechanically, the Mustang II differed in many ways from the first generation Mustangs. The front suspension was redesigned. The front springs were now located between the control arms rather than above the upper A arm. A front subframe was designed to isolate the engine from the rest of the chassis mostly due to the inherent vibration of the standard 2.3L four-cylinder engine. Rack and pinion replaced the recirculating ball steering, and front disc brakes were standard, as were staggered rear shocks. Also standard equipment was a four-speed manual transmission.

In the interior, a more informative dash was used. Tachometer, fuel, alternator and temperature gauges were standard as were non-reclining bucket seats.

Two engines were available. The base 140 ci 2.3L four-cylinder was the first metric American engine. It featured a cross-flow single overhead cam cylinder head, but it pumped out a meager 88 hp—not really enough for a Mustang weighing close to 3,000 pounds.

The only optional engine for 1974 was the German-built 171 ci 2.8L V-6 rated at 105 hp. It was a nice little engine, but again the Mustang II was too heavy for any sort of performance that was reminiscent of the first generation Mustangs.

The Mustang II was available in three models, base in either hardtop or three-door 2+2, the luxury-oriented two-door hardtop Ghia and the performance looking Mach 1 three-door 2+2.

The Ghia moniker replaced the Grande and was the luxury Mustang. Ghia was the name of the Italian design studios that Ford had acquired. Using the Ghia name was intended to lend an air of European exclusivity. The Ghia came with the expected upgrades: deluxe seatbelts, digital quartz clock, the luxury interior group (vinyl seats and door trim, door courtesy lights, 25-oz carpeting, rear ashtray, parking brake boot and sound package), outside color-keyed remote control mirrors, pin stripes, vinyl roof, Picardy velour cloth and the styled steel wheels were a no-cost option.

The Mach 1 came with the larger engine, the 2.8L V-6, and a unique lower bodyside treatment with Mach 1 lettering. However, the Rallye package was required to give the Mach 1 the maximum performance potential. The package consisted of the Traction-Lok differential, CR70x13 wide oval radial B/WL tires, extra cooling package, digital quartz clock, the Competition Suspension (heavy-duty front and rear springs, rear stabilizer bar and adjustable shocks), outside color-keyed remote control mirrors, leather-wrapped steering wheel and styled steel wheels/trim rings.

Other interesting options were a manual sunroof, forged aluminum wheels and an anti-theft alarm system.

*1974 three-door* Ford Motor Co.

# Chapter 11

# 1975 Mustang II

## Production Figures

| | | | |
|---|---|---|---|
| 60F 2dr Hardtop | 85,155 | 69R 3dr Hatchback | |
| 69F 3dr Hatchback | 30,038 | Mach 1 | 21,062 |
| 60H 2dr Hardtop Ghia | 52,320 | Total | 188,575 |

## Serial Numbers

5F03Y100001

5 — Last digit of model year

F — Assembly plant (F-Dearborn, R-San Jose, T-Metuchen)

03 — Plate code for Mustang (02-2dr hardtop, 03-3dr hatchback, 04-2dr hardtop Ghia, 05-3dr hatchback Mach 1)

Y — Engine code

100001 — Consecutive unit number

### Location

Stamped on plate riveted to driver's side of dash; certification label attached to rear face of driver's door.

### Engine Codes

Y — 140 ci 2.3L 2V 4 cyl 88 hp

Z — 171 ci 2.8L 2V V-6 105 hp

F — 302 ci 5.0L 2V V-8 140 hp

## 1975 Mustang II Prices

| | Retail |
|---|---|
| 4 cyl 2.3 liter Models | |
| 2dr Hardtop, 60F | $3,529.00 |
| 3dr 2+2, 69F | 3,818.00 |
| 2dr Ghia, 60H | 3,938.00 |
| 6 cyl 2.8 liter Model | |
| 3dr Mach 1, 69R | 4,188.00 |
| 2.8 liter V-6 6 cyl (NA with SelectShift) | 272.00 |
| 302 cid 2V 8 cyl | |
| Mach 1 (includes SelectShift transmission) | 203.00 |
| All others | 217.00 |
| Credit for 2.3 liter substitution from base 2.8 V-6 | (272.00) |
| SelectShift Cruise-O-Matic | 239.00 |
| Accent Group, exterior | 162.00 |
| Air conditioner, SelectAire | 417.00 |
| Anti-theft alarm system | 76.00 |
| Axle, Traction-Lok differential | 46.00 |
| Battery, heavy-duty 53 ampere | 14.00 |
| Seatbelts, color-keyed deluxe | 17.00 |
| Brakes, power front disc | 55.00 |
| Bumper guards, front & rear | 35.00 |
| Clock, digital quartz crystal | 40.00 |

| | |
|---|---|
| Console | 63.00 |
| Convenience Group (depending on model) | 7.00–70.00 |
| Defroster, electric rear window | 63.00 |
| Emission equipment, Calif. | 41.00 |
| Fuel tank, extended range (std. 302 V–8) | 19.00 |
| Glass, tinted complete | 41.00 |
| Light Group | 35.00 |
| Light, fuel monitor warning | 19.00 |
| Lock Group, security | 15.00 |
| Luxury Interior Group, Hardtop | 106.00 |
| 3dr 2+2 and Mach 1 | 89.00 |
| Luxury Group, Ghia Silver | 162.00 |
| Maintenance Group | 48.00 |
| Mirrors, outside dual color-keyed | 39.00 |
| Molding, rocker panel | 19.00 |
| Molding, color-keyed vinyl insert bodyside | 51.00 |
| Moonroof, silver glass | 454.00 |
| Paint, glamour | 49.00 |
| Protection Group, Mach 1 | 20.00 |
| All others | 29.00 |
| Radio, AM | 65.00 |
| Radio, AM/FM monaural | 136.00 |
| Radio, AM/FM stereo | 225.00 |
| Radio with tape player, AM/FM stereo | 347.00 |
| Rallye Package, Mach 1 | 141.00 |
| 3dr 2+2 | 195.00 |
| All others | 282.00 |
| Roof, vinyl | 83.00 |
| Roof, vinyl half, Ghia | N/C |
| Seat, fold down rear (std. 3dr) | 66.00 |
| Steering, power rack & pinion | 117.00 |
| Steering wheel, leather-wrapped | 32.00 |
| Stripes, pin | 24.00 |
| Sunroof, manually operated | 210.00 |
| Suspension, Competition, Ghia & Accent Group | 43.00 |
| Mach 1 | 25.00 |
| All others | 55.00 |
| Trim, velour cloth, Ghia | 88.00 |
| Trim rings | 35.00 |
| Wheels, four cast aluminum spoke | |
| Mach 1, Rallye Package, 3dr 2+2 with Exterior Accent Group | 78.00 |
| 3dr 2+2 or Hardtop with Exterior Accent Group | 113.00 |
| Ghia | 113.00 |
| Hardtop without Exterior Accent Group | 158.00 |
| Wheels, four styled steel, Ghia | N/C |
| Hardtop | 45.00 |
| Windows, pivoting rear quarter(3dr) | 33.00 |
| Credit for deletion of color-keyed deluxe seatbelts | (17.00) |
| Credit for deletion of digital clock | (40.00) |
| Credit for deletion of tinted glass-complete | (41.00) |
| Typical tire upgrade | 30.00–105.00 |

## 1975 Exterior Colors

| Colors | Code |
|---|---|
| Black | 1C |
| Silver Metallic | 1G |
| Bright Red | 2B |
| Dark Red | 2M |
| Bright Blue Metallic | 3E |
| Silver Blue Glow | 3M |
| Pastel Blue | 3Q |
| Green Glow | 4T |
| Dark Yellow Green Metallic | 4V |
| Light Green | 47 |
| Medium Copper Metallic | 5M |
| Dark Brown Metallic | 5Q |
| Tan Glow | 5U |
| Bright Yellow | 6E |
| Polar White | 9D |

## 1975 Interior Trim

| Trim | Code |
|---|---|
| Black | A |
| Blue | B |
| Red | D |
| Green | G |
| Cranberry | H |
| White/Red | N |
| White/Blue | Q |
| Tan | U |
| White/Tan | 4 |
| White/Green | 5 |

## 1975 Mustang Facts

The 1975 Mustang II was hardly changed. The grille got a larger eggcrate-type mesh, which was now practically flush with the grille opening, and the Ghia model came with opera windows to enhance its luxury image.

The 2.3L four-cylinder engine was still standard equipment, with the 2.8L V-6 optional, again available only with a four-speed manual. The 302 ci V-8 rated at 140 hp became optional on all Mustangs.

The Ghia Luxury Group, optional on the Ghia, included silver metallic paint, a half vinyl roof in Silver Normande grain, full-length bodyside tape stripes, stand-up hood ornament, media velour cloth trim in cranberry, console, flocked headlining and sun visor.

There was also the regular Luxury Interior Group (standard on the Ghia) which included a choice of vinyl or cloth and vinyl seat trim, deluxe door and rear seat quarter trim, door courtesy lights, color-keyed deluxe belts on hardtops, shag carpeting, rear ashtray, parking brake boot and, as Ford called it, a super sound package.

Two sunroofs were available, the silver glass moonroof and the regular version, both manually controlled.

The Rallye Package, available only with the 2.8 V-6 or the 302 V-8, tightened the chassis up a bit for better handling. It included the Traction-Lok differential, 195/70 BWL tires, extra cooling package, exhaust with bright tips, digital clock (hardtops), the Competition Suspension, remote control outside color-keyed mirrors, leather-wrapped steering wheel and styled steel wheels with trim rings.

The Competition Suspension, available by itself, included heavy-duty springs, Gabriel adjustable shocks, a rear stabilizer bar and 195/70x13 B/WL tires.

From the performance point of view, the availability of the 302 ci V-8 helped give the Mustang II a much needed shot in the arm. Available only with the three-speed automatic transmission, mandatory options were power brakes and steering. California-bound

302s got catalytic converters and all Mustang engines benefited from electronic ignition.

Steel-belted radial tires were now standard equipment.

New wheels became available. These were a cast aluminum spoke-type wheel. The styled steel and forged aluminum wheels were also available.

Late in the model year, an MPG version of the Mustang II was made available. Using the 2.3L four-cylinder engine and a lower numerical rear axle ratio, 3.18:1 vs 3.40:1, the MPG Mustang was designed to deliver better mileage. New lows were reached in terms of acceleration.

*1975 two-door Ghia*

# Chapter 12

# 1976 Mustang II

## Production Figures

| | | | |
|---|---|---|---|
| 60F 2dr Hardtop | 78,508 | 69R 3dr Hatchback | |
| 69F 3dr Hatchback | 62,312 | Mach 1 | 9,232 |
| 60H 2dr Hardtop Ghia | 37,515 | Total | 187,567 |

## Serial Numbers

6F03Y100001

6 — Last digit of model year

F — Assembly plant (F-Dearborn, R-San Jose)

03 — Plate code for Mustang (02-2dr hardtop, 03-3dr hatchback, 04-2dr hardtop Ghia, 05-3dr hatchback Mach 1)

Y — Engine code

100001 — Consecutive unit number

### Location

Stamped on plate riveted on driver's side of dash; certification label attached to rear face of driver's door.

### Engine Codes

Y — 140 ci 2.3L 2V 4 cyl 88 hp

Z — 171 ci 2.8L 2V V-6 105 hp

F — 302 ci 5.0L 2V V-8 140 hp

## 1976 Mustang II Prices

| | Retail |
|---|---|
| 4 cyl 2.3 liter Models | |
|    MPG 2dr Hardtop, 60F | $3,525.00 |
|    MPG 3dr 2+2, 69F | 3,781.00 |
|    MPG 2dr Ghia, 60H | 3,859.00 |
| 6 cyl 2.8 liter Models | |
|    2dr Hardtop, 60F | 3,791.00 |
|    3dr 2+2, 69F | 4,047.00 |
|    2dr Ghia, 60H | 4,125.00 |
|    3dr Mach 1, 69R | 4,209.00 |
| 8 cyl 302 cid Models | |
|    2dr Hardtop, 60F | 3,737.00 |
|    3dr 2+2, 69F | 3,992.00 |
|    2dr Ghia, 60H | 4,071.00 |
|    3dr Mach 1, 69R | 4,154.00 |
| Credit for 2.3 liter substitution on Mach 1 | (272.00) |
| 4-speed manual heavy-duty transmission (required with 302 cid unless Cruise-O-Matic is ordered) | 37.00 |
| SelectShift Cruise-O-Matic | 239.00 |
| Accent Group, exterior | 169.00 |
| Air conditioner, SelectAire (requires power steering) | 420.00 |
| Anti-theft alarm system | 83.00 |

| | |
|---|---:|
| Axle, optional ratio | 13.00 |
| Axle, Traction-Lok differential (requires power front disc brakes) | 48.00 |
| Battery, heavy-duty (std. 2.8 & 302 cid) | 14.00 |
| Seatbelts, deluxe color-keyed | 17.00 |
| Black Midnight option (Mach 1 only) | 83.00 |
| Bracket, front license plate | N/C |
| Brakes, power front disc | 54.00 |
| Bumper guards, front & rear | 34.00 |
| Clock, digital quartz crystal | 40.00 |
| Clock, electric (NA w/Rallye Package) | 17.00 |
| Cobra II Package | 325.00 |
| Cobra II Modification Package | 287.00 |
| Console | 71.00 |
| Convenience Group | 35.00 |
| Defroster, electric rear window | 70.00 |
| Emission equipment, Calif. | 49.00 |
| Fuel tank, extended range | 24.00 |
| Ghia Luxury Group | 177.00 |
| Glass, tinted complete | 46.00 |
| Heater, engine block | 17.00 |
| Horn, dual note | 6.00 |
| Light Group, models with sunroof or moonroof | 28.00 |
| All others | 41.00 |
| Light, fuel monitor warning | 18.00 |
| Lock Group, security | 16.00 |
| Luggage rack, deck lid | 51.00 |
| Luxury Interior Group | 117.00 |
| Mirrors, outside dual color-keyed | 42.00 |
| Molding, color-keyed vinyl insert bodyside | 60.00 |
| Molding, rocker panel | 19.00 |
| Moonroof, glass | 470.00 |
| Paint, glamour | 54.00 |
| Paint/tape, Tu-tone | 84.00 |
| Protection Group, Mach 1 & models w/Black Midnight option | 36.00 |
| All others | 43.00 |
| Radio, AM | 71.00 |
| Radio with tape player, AM | 192.00 |
| Radio, AM/FM monaural | 128.00 |
| Radio, AM/FM stereo | 299.00 |
| Rallye Package, Mach 1 & w/Cobra II | 163.00 |
| All others | 237.00 |
| Roof, vinyl | 86.00 |
| Roof, half vinyl, Ghia only | N/C |
| Seat, fold-down rear (std. 3dr) | 72.00 |
| Stallion Group, Hardtop & 2+2 | 72.00 |
| Steering, power rack & pinion (required with 302 cid & 2.8 liter w/air conditioning; power front disc brakes also required) | 117.00 |
| Steering wheel, leather-wrapped | 33.00 |
| Stripes, pin | 27.00 |

| | |
|---|---|
| Sunroof, manually operated | 230.00 |
| Suspension, Competition | 29.00 |
| Trim, velour cloth, Ghia only | 99.00 |
| Trim rings | 35.00 |
| Wheels, four cast aluminum spoke | |
|   Mach 1, Rallye Package or Cobra II | 96.00 |
|   Ghia, Stallion Group or Exterior Accent Group | 131.00 |
|   All others | 182.00 |
| Wheels, four forged aluminum | |
|   Mach 1, Rallye Package or Cobra II | 96.00 |
|   Ghia, Stallion Group or Exterior Accent Group | 131.00 |
|   All others | 182.00 |
| Wheels, four styled steel | |
|   Hardtop & 2+2 | 51.00 |
|   Ghia | N/C |
| Windows, pivoting rear | 33.00 |
| Fleet options: | |
|   Light, luggage compartment | 4.00 |
|   Mirror, lefthand color-keyed | 14.00 |
|   Tinted glass, windshield | 24.00 |
|   Tire upgrade | 33.00–208.00 |

## 1976 Exterior Colors

| | Code |
|---|---|
| Black | 1C |
| Silver Metallic | 1G |
| Bright Red | 2B |
| Dark Red | 2M |
| Bright Blue Metallic | 3E |
| Silver Blue Glow | 3M |
| Medium Ivy Bronze Metallic | 4T |
| Dark Yellow Green Metallic | 4V |
| Light Green | 47 |
| Medium Chestnut Metallic | 5M |
| Dark Brown Metallic | 5Q |
| Tan Glow | 5U |
| Bright Yellow | 6E |
| Polar White | 9D |

## Tu-tone Exterior Color Combinations

| Body color/accent color | Code |
|---|---|
| Cream/Medium Gold Metallic | 6P/6V |
| White/Bright Red | 9D/2R |
| White/Bright Blue Metallic | 9D/3E |

## 1976 Interior Trim

| | Code |
|---|---|
| Black | A |
| Blue | B |
| Red | D |
| Cranberry | H |
| Aqua | K |
| Tan | U |
| White/Red | N |
| White/Blue | Q |
| White/Tan | 4 |
| White/Black | W |

## 1976 Mustang II Facts

The 1976 Mustang II continued with few changes. Most options and packages were carried over from 1975.

Base Mustang models with the 2.3 were all classified as MPG models, stressing their economy features.

The 2.8L V-6 was now available with an automatic transmission, at extra cost.

A wide ratio four-speed manual became available on the 302 V-8.

The Stallion Group, coinciding with similar offerings on the Maverick and Pinto, was strictly a cosmetic package. It included black greenhouse moldings and wiper arms, black grille (horse grille emblem deleted), black rocker panels, lower fenders, lower doors, lower front and rear bumpers, and black lower quarter panels. Also included were four styled steel wheels, bright lower bodyside moldings and Stallion decals. The wheel lip moldings were deleted.

The Cobra II modification package was installed by Motortown Corporation. It included: a front air spoiler, rear deck lid spoiler and simulated hood scoop; quarter window louvers with "snake" emblems; accent stripes on front spoiler, hood, roof, rear deck, rear deck spoiler and lower bodyside panels; "snake" emblems on the fenders and wheel centers; and a "snake" emblem on the blacked-out grille.

Paint schemes were white with blue stripes or black and gold stripes. All Mustang engines were available, but it was the 302 V-8 that helped fullfill the promises made by the Cobra II package.

*1976 three-door Stallion*

# Chapter 13

# 1977 Mustang II

## Production Figures

| | | | |
|---|---|---|---|
| 60F 2dr Hardtop | 67,783 | 69R 3dr Hatchback | |
| 69F 3dr Hatchback | 49,161 | Mach 1 | 6,719 |
| 60H 2dr Hardtop Ghia | 29,510 | Total | 153,173 |

## Serial Numbers

7F03Y100001

7 — Last digit of model year

F — Assembly plant (F-Dearborn, R-San Jose)

03 — Plate code for Mustang (02-2dr Hardtop, 03-3dr Hatchback, 04-2dr Hardtop Ghia, 05-3dr Hatchback Mach 1)

Y — Engine code

100001 — Consecutive unit number

### Location

Stamped on plate riveted on driver's side of dash, visible through the windshield; certification label attached on rear face of driver's door.

### Engine Codes

Y — 140 ci 2.3L 2V 4 cyl 92 hp

Z — 171 ci 2.8L 2V V-6 103 hp

F — 302 ci 5.0L 2V V-8 134 hp

## 1977 Mustang II Prices

| | Retail |
|---|---|
| 4 cyl 2.3 liter Models | |
| 2dr Hardtop, 60F | $3,678.00 |
| 3dr 2+2, 69F | 3,877.00 |
| 2dr Ghia, 60H | 4,096.00 |
| 6 cyl 2.8 liter Models | |
| 3dr Mach 1, 69R | 4,332.00 |
| Credit for 2.3 liter substitution on Mach 1 | (306.00) |
| 2.8 liter 6 cyl | 306.00 |
| 302 cid 8 cyl, Mach 1 | (12.00) |
| All others | 294.00 |
| SelectShift Cruise-O-Matic (required with 302 cid) | 248.00 |
| Four-speed manual (NA 302 cid) | N/C |
| Appearance Decor Group (NA Mach 1, Ghia, Cobra II) | |
| Hardtop | 151.00 |
| 2+2 | 106.00 |
| Accent Group, exterior, Hardtop | 211.00 |
| Air conditioner, SelectAire | 443.00 |
| Seatbelts, color-keyed deluxe | 17.00 |
| Brakes, power front disc | 57.00 |
| Bumper guards, front & rear | 35.00 |

| | |
|---|---:|
| Clock, digital quartz crystal | 42.00 |
| Cloth & vinyl bucket seats, Hardtop & 2+2 | 12.00 |
| Cobra II Package | 689.00 |
| Console | 75.00 |
| Convenience Group, 3dr (NA Cobra II & T-roof) | 65.00 |
| All others | 33.00 |
| Defroster, electric rear window | 70.00 |
| Fold-down rear seat (std. 3dr) | 84.00 |
| Ghia Sports Group (Ghia only) | 398.00 |
| Luxury Interior Group | 147.00 |
| Glass, tinted complete | 49.00 |
| T-roof convertible option (2+2 & Mach 1) | |
| 2+2 with Cobra II | 587.00 |
| All others | 629.00 |
| Light Group, w/manually operated sunroof, | |
| flip-up open air roof & T-roof | 37.00 |
| All others | 42.00 |
| Luggage rack, deck lid | 52.00 |
| Mirrors, dual sport | 47.00 |
| Moldings, color-keyed vinyl insert bodyside | 63.00 |
| Moldings, rocker panel | 20.00 |
| Bodyside molding color-keyed to exterior paint | N/C |
| Stripes, pin | 28.00 |
| Protection Group | |
| Models w/front license plate bracket | |
| Mach 1 & Cobra II | 27.00 |
| All others | 34.00 |
| Models without bracket | |
| Mach 1 & Cobra II | 23.00 |
| All others | 30.00 |
| Radio, AM | 65.00 |
| Radio with stereo tape player, AM | 192.00 |
| Radio, AM/FM monaural | 120.00 |
| Radio, AM/FM stereo, models | |
| with Deluxe Equipment Group | 41.00 |
| All others | 161.00 |
| Radio with tape player, AM/FM stereo | |
| Models with Deluxe Equipment Group | 108.00 |
| All others | 229.00 |
| Rallye Appearance Package, 2+2 | 157.00 |
| Rallye Package, Mach 1, Cobra II, Exterior Accent Group | |
| & Rallye Appearance Package | 54.00 |
| All others | 101.00 |
| Seat, 4-way manual driver's | 30.00 |
| Sports Performance Package, includes 302 cid V-8 | |
| heavy-duty 4-speed manual transmission, | |
| power steering, power brakes and 195/70R WSW | |
| (RWL on 2+2 & Mach 1) tires | |
| Hardtop with Exterior Accent Group | 649.00 |
| Hardtop without Exterior Accent Group | 686.00 |
| 2+2 model with Cobra II package | 516.00 |
| 2+2 without Cobra II package | 649.00 |

| | |
|---|---|
| Ghia | 593.00 |
| Mach 1 | 210.00 |
| Discount, Mach 1 | (122.00) |
| All others | (135.00) |
| Steering, power rack & pinion | 125.00 |
| Steering wheel, leather-wrapped sport | |
| 2+2 & Mach 1 | 35.00 |
| All others | 51.00 |
| Trim, media velour cloth, Ghia only | 102.00 |
| Roof, flip-up open air, 2dr only | 145.00 |
| Sunroof, manually operated, 2dr only | 237.00 |
| Roof, full vinyl, Hardtop only | 88.00 |
| Paint, metallic glow | 57.00 |
| Trim rings, 2+2 only | 36.00 |
| Wheel covers, wire, Hardtop | 82.00 |
| 2+2 | 40.00 |
| Ghia | 63.00 |
| Mach 1, Cobra II, Exterior Accent Group, Appearance Decor Group or Rallye Appearance Package | 4.00 |
| Wheels, four lacy spoke aluminum (NA Ghia Sports Group) | |
| Hardtop | 204.00 |
| 2+2 | 161.00 |
| Ghia | 184.00 |
| Mach 1, Cobra II, Exterior Accent Group, Appearance Decor Group or Rallye Appearance Package | 125.00 |
| Wheels, four forged aluminum (NA Ghia Sports Group) | |
| Hardtop | 204.00 |
| 2+2 | 161.00 |
| Ghia | 184.00 |
| Mach 1, Cobra II, Exterior Accent Group, Appearance Decor Group or Rallye Appearance Package | 125.00 |
| Wheels, four white lacy spoke aluminum (NA Ghia Sports Group or Rallye Appearance Package) | |
| Hardtop | 252.00 |
| 2+2 | 210.00 |
| Ghia | 233.00 |
| Mach 1, Cobra II, Exterior Accent Group or Appearance Decor Group | 173.00 |
| Wheels with trim rings, four styled steel (std. with Mach 1 and 2+2 [less trim rings]), Exterior Accent Group, Appearance Decor Group and Rallye Appearance Package) | |
| Hardtop | 78.00 |
| Ghia | 59.00 |
| Spoiler, front, 2+2 and Mach 1 | N/C |
| Battery, heavy-duty | 16.00 |
| Bracket, front license plate | N/C |
| High altitude emission equipment | 22.00 |
| Emission equipment, Calif. | 69.00 |
| Tires, typical upgrade | 18.00–185.00 |

Limited production options

| | |
|---|---|
| Heater, engine block immersion | 18.00 |
| Light, luggage compartment | 4.00 |
| Mirror, inside day/night | 7.00 |

Fleet options

| | |
|---|---|
| Mirror, lefthand sport | 14.00 |
| Tinted glass, windshield | 24.00 |

## 1977 Exterior Colors

| Colors | Code |
|---|---|
| Black | 1C |
| Bright Red | 2R |
| Dark Brown Metallic | 5Q |
| Bright Yellow | 6E |
| Cream | 6P |
| Golden Glow | 6V |
| Bright Aqua Glow | 7H |
| Light Aqua Metallic | 7Q |
| Medium Emerald Glow | 7S |
| Orange | 8G |
| Tan | 8H |
| Bright Saddle Metallic | 8K |
| Polar White | 9D |

## Tu-tone Exterior Color Combinations*

| Body color/accent color | Code |
|---|---|
| Cream/Medium Gold Metallic | 6P/6V |

## 1977 Exterior Colors

| Colors | Code |
|---|---|
| White/Bright Red | 9D/2R |
| White/Light Aqua Metallic | 9D/7Q |

*Before 6-27-77; after, see 1978

## 1977 Interior Trim*

| | Code |
|---|---|
| Black | A |
| Red | D |
| Aqua | K |
| Chamois | T |
| Cream | V |
| White/Red | N |
| White/Black | W |
| White/Chamois | 2 |
| White/Emerald | 5 |
| White/Aqua | 7 |
| White/Gold | 8 |

*Before 6-27-77; after, see 1978

## 1977 Mustang II Facts

In 1977, two-door models got a new horizontal grille while all SportsRoof Mustangs came with a blacked-out grille.

SportsRoofs were also upgraded by the addition of a standard sport steering wheel, styled steel wheels with raised white letters, bias belted tires and brushed aluminum instrument panel appliques. Hardtops came with pecan-colored woodgrain appliques.

A new interior option was the four-way adjustable seats. These were adjustable for height in addition to forward and back. The seatback was still non-adjustable.

The front spoiler used on the Cobra II was available on all SportsRoofs as a no-cost option.

The moonroof was deleted but the regular manually-controlled sunroof remained. A flip-up open air roof was also available. It either flipped up in the rear, or could be removed completely.

1977 was the first year for the T-roof option, consisting of removable roof panels, but it was only available on the three-door models.

The Appearance Decor Group, not available on the Ghia or Mach 1, included lower body Tu-tone paint treatment, pin stripes, four styled steel wheels with trim rings, all vinyl or cloth and vinyl seat trim, and brushed aluminum instrument panel appliques. Wheel lip moldings were deleted.

Available only on hardtops was the Exterior Accent Group, consisting of pin stripes, wide color-keyed vinyl insert bodyside moldings, WSW tires, dual sport mirrors and four styled steel wheels with trim rings.

Complementing the Rallye Package was a Rallye Appearance Package, available only on the three-door. It was primarily a blacked-out treatment.

The Sports Performance Package consisted of the 302 ci V-8 engine, four-speed manual transmission, power steering and brakes, and 195/70R WSW tires.

Available only on the Ghia was the unique Ghia Sports Group. It consisted of black or tan exterior paint, chamois or black half-vinyl roof, vinyl insert bodyside moldings, pin stripes, luggage rack with black or chamois hold-down straps with bright buckles, lacy spoke aluminum wheels with chamois painted spokes and blacked-out grille. In the interior, the Ghia seat trim was finished in chamois with black upper straps on the seatbacks, black engine-turned applique inserts on the instrument panel, console tray-door, trim panel inserts, console, leather-wrapped steering wheel, black shift lever with manual transmission and black parking brake handle.

The Ghia Silver Luxury Group was deleted for 1977.

Performance image duties were still handled by the Mach 1 and SportsRoof with the Cobra II package. Two additional stripe colors, red and green, were available on white Cobra IIs. All 1977 and later Cobra IIs were built by Ford.

California-bound 2.8L V-6s and 302 ci V-8s were equipped with a new Variable-Venturi carburetor design.

The cast aluminum spoke wheels were deleted. Lacy spoke wheels in natural or painted white became options.

*1977 Cobra II* Joy Jacobs

# Chapter 14

# 1978 Mustang II

## Production Figures

| | | | |
|---|---|---|---|
| 60F 2dr Hardtop | 81,304 | 69R 3dr Hatchback | |
| 69F 3dr Hatchback | 68,408 | Mach 1 | 7,968 |
| 60H 2dr Hardtop Ghia | 34,730 | Total | 192,410 |

## Serial Numbers

8F03Y100001

8 — Last digit of model year

F — Assembly plant (F-Dearborn, R-San Jose)

03 — Plate code for Mustang (02-2dr hardtop, 03-3dr hatchback, 04-2dr hardtop Ghia, 05-3dr hatchback Mach 1)

Y — Engine code

100001 — Consecutive unit number

### Location

Stamped on plate riveted on driver's side of dash, visible through the windshield; certification label attached on rear face of driver's door.

### Engine Codes

Y — 140 ci 2.3L 2V 4 cyl 88 hp

Z — 171 ci 2.8L 2V V-6 90 hp

F — 302 ci 5.0L 2V V-8 139 hp

## 1978 Mustang II Prices

| | Retail |
|---|---|
| 2.3 liter 4 cyl Models | |
|    2dr Hardtop | $3,824.00 |
|    3dr 2+2 | 4,088.00 |
|    2dr Ghia | 4,242.00 |
| 2.8 liter 6 cyl Models | |
|    3dr Mach 1 | 4,523.00 |
|      Credit for 2.3 liter substitution from 2.8 liter, | |
|      Mach 1 | (237.00) |
| 2.8 liter 2V 6 cyl (Variable Venturi in Calif.) | 237.00 |
| 5.0 liter (302 cid) 8 cyl | |
|    Mach 1 | 148.00 |
|    All others | 386.00 |
| SelectShift Cruise-O-Matic | 292.00 |
| Accent Group, Exterior | |
|    Hardtop | 245.00 |
|    2+2 | 163.00 |
| Air conditioner, SelectAire | 469.00 |
| Appearance Decor Group | |
|    Hardtop | 167.00 |
|    2+2 | 128.00 |
| Seatbelts, color-keyed deluxe | 19.00 |

| | |
|---|---:|
| Bodyside protection, lower | 30.00 |
| Bracket, front license plate | N/C |
| Brakes, power front disc | 66.00 |
| Bumper guards, front and rear | 39.00 |
| Clock, digital quartz crystal | 46.00 |
| Cobra II Package | |
|     Models with 2.3 or 2.8 liter engine | 701.00 |
|     Models with 5.0 liter engine | 724.00 |
| Console | 75.00 |
| Convenience Group | |
|     3dr, except Cobra II or T-roof | 81.00 |
|     All others | 34.00 |
| Defroster, electric rear window | 80.00 |
| Emission equipment, Calif. | 69.00 |
| Emission equipment, high altitude | 33.00 |
| Fashion Accessory Package | 219.00 |
| Fold-down rear seat | 90.00 |
| Ghia Sports Group | 386.00 |
| Glass, tinted complete | 54.00 |
| Heater, engine block immersion | 12.00 |
| Illuminated entry system | 49.00 |
| King Cobra option | 1,277.00 |
| Light Group | |
|     Models with flip-up roof or T-roof | 40.00 |
|     All others | 52.00 |
| Luxury Interior Group | |
|     Hardtop | 167.00 |
|     2+2 and Mach 1 | 161.00 |
| Mirror, lefthand illuminated visor vanity | 34.00 |
| Mirrors, dual sport | 49.00 |
| Moldings, color-keyed vinyl insert bodyside | 66.00 |
| Moldings, bodyside color-keyed to exterior paint | N/C |
| Moldings, rocker panel | 22.00 |
| Paint, metallic glow | 40.00 |
| Protection Group | |
|     Models with front license plate bracket | |
|         Mach 1 | 28.00 |
|         All others | 36.00 |
|     Models without front license plate bracket | |
|         Mach 1 | 24.00 |
|         All others | 33.00 |
| Radio flexibility option | 90.00 |
| Radio, AM | 72.00 |
| Radio with 8-track stereo tape player, AM | 192.00 |
| Radio, AM/FM monaural | 120.00 |
| Radio, AM/FM stereo | 161.00 |
| Radio with cassette player, AM/FM stereo | 229.00 |
| Radio with 8-track tape player, AM/FM stereo | 229.00 |
| Rallye Appearance Package | 163.00 |
| Rallye Package | |
|     Mach 1, Exterior Accent Group, | |
|     Rallye Appearance Package | 43.00 |

| | |
|---|---:|
| All others | 93.00 |
| Roof, flip-up open air | 167.00 |
| Roof, full vinyl | 99.00 |
| Seat, 4-way manual driver's | 33.00 |
| Spoiler, front | 8.00 |
| Steering, power rack & pinion | 134.00 |
| Steering wheel, leather-wrapped sport | |
|   2+2, Mach 1 | 34.00 |
|   All others | 49.00 |
| Stripes, pin | 30.00 |
| T-roof convertible option | |
|   2+2 without Cobra II, Mach 1 | 689.00 |
|   2+2 with Cobra II | 647.00 |
| Trim, cloth & vinyl (Ashton cloth) | 12.00 |
| Trim, Willshire cloth | 100.00 |
| Trim rings | 39.00 |
| Wheel covers, wire | |
|   Hardtop | 96.00 |
|   2+2 | 45.00 |
|   Ghia | 77.00 |
|   Mach 1, Cobra II, Exterior Accent Group, Appearance Decor Group, Rallye Appearance Package | 12.00 |
| Wheels, four lacy spoke aluminum | |
|   Hardtop | 276.00 |
|   2+2 | 224.00 |
|   Ghia | 257.00 |
|   Mach 1, Cobra II, Exterior Accent Group, Appearance Decor Group, Rallye Appearance Package | 186.00 |
| Wheels, four forged aluminum | |
|   Hardtop | 276.00 |
|   2+2 | 224.00 |
|   Ghia | 257.00 |
|   Mach 1, Cobra II, Exterior Accent Group, Appearance Decor Group, Rallye Appearance Package | 186.00 |
| Wheels, four white lacy spoke aluminum | |
|   Hardtop | 289.00 |
|   2+2 | 237.00 |
|   Ghia | 270.00 |
|   Mach 1, Cobra II, Exterior Accent Group, Appearance Decor Group, Rallye Appearance Package | 199.00 |
| Wheels with trim rings, four white styled steel | |
|   Hardtop | 90.00 |
|   Ghia | 71.00 |
| Wheels, four white painted forged aluminum | |
|   Hardtop | 289.00 |
|   2+2 | 237.00 |
|   Ghia | 270.00 |
|   Mach 1, Cobra II, Exterior Accent Group, Appearance Decor Group, Rallye Appearance Package | 199.00 |

| Typical tire upgrade | 23.00–202.00 |
|---|---|
| Limited Production options | |
| Light, luggage compartment | 4.00 |
| Mirror, inside day/night | 7.00 |
| Mirror, lefthand color-keyed sport | 16.00 |
| Tinted glass, windshield | 25.00 |

## 1978 Exterior Colors

| Color | Code |
|---|---|
| Black | 1C |
| Silver Metallic | 1G |
| Bright Red | 2R |
| Dark Midnight Blue | 3A |
| Dark Jade Metallic | 46 |
| Medium Chestnut Metallic | 5M |
| Dark Brown Metallic | 5Q |
| Bright Yellow | 6E |
| Aqua Glow | 7H |
| Aqua Metallic | 7Q |
| Chamois Glow | 8W |
| Light Chamois | 83 |
| Tangerine | 85 |
| Polar White | 9D |

## Tu-tone Exterior Color Combinations

| Body color/accent color | Code |
|---|---|
| Silver Metallic/ Black | 1G/1C |
| Silver Metallic/ Bright Red | 1G/2R |
| Bright Red/Black | 2R/1C |
| Bright Red/White | 2R/9D |
| Dark Jade Metallic/ White | 46/9D |

## Tu-tone Exterior Color Combinations

| Combination | Code |
|---|---|
| Bright Yellow/Black | 6E/1C |
| Bright Aqua Metallic/White | 7H/9D |
| Light Aqua Metallic/ White | 7Q/9D |
| Light Chamois/ Medium Chestnut Metallic | 83/5M |
| Tangerine/White | 85/9D |
| White/Black | 9D/1C |
| White/Bright Red | 9D/2R |
| White/Aqua Metallic | 9D/7Q |

## 1978 Interior Trim

| Trim | Code |
|---|---|
| Black | A |
| Red | D |
| Tangerine | J |
| Aqua | K |
| White/Red | N |
| Chamois | T |
| White/Black | W |
| White/Chamois | 2 |
| White/Aqua | 7 |
| White/Gold | 8 |

## 1978 Mustang II Facts

1978 was the last year for the Mustang II, the Mach 1 model and the Cobra II option package.

In the interior, the most noticeable change was the use of two rear seat cushions replacing the previous full-length seat.

Mechanically, the 302 ci V-8 came with either a two-barrel or the Variable Venturi carburetor. The optional power steering was enhanced through the use of variable ratio.

The Cobra II got a new tape stripe treatment, and black rear window louvers, similar to the Sport Slats of 1969–70 Mustangs, were made part of the package.

The Fashion Accessory Package, specifically designed to appeal to women, consisted of Fresno cloth seat inserts, a driver's side illuminated sun visor mirror (useful in slow traffic), a four-way adjustable driver's seat, coin tray, map pockets for maps and other things, an illuminated entry system and exterior tape stripes.

The optional styled steel wheels with trim rings were available in white only. The forged aluminum wheels were also available in white, in addition to natural aluminum.

The most expensive option seen on the Mustang since the Boss 429 engine was the King Cobra option, at $1,277.00. This was a special cosmetic treatment/equipment package for the Sports-Roof. It included a special front air dam, the Cobra II's hood scoop and rear spoiler, wheels similar to those found on the Pontiac Trans AM, special striping and hood decal, and King Cobra identification. Mechanically, the 302 ci V-8 was standard equipment as was power steering, power brakes, heavy-duty springs, adjustable shocks, rear stabilizer bar and spoke wheels.

*1978 Cobra II* Ford Motor Co.

*1978 King Cobra*

# Chapter 15

# 1979 Mustang

## Production Figures

| | | | |
|---|---|---|---|
| 66B 2dr Sedan | 156,666 | 61H 3dr Hatchback | |
| 61R 3dr Hatchback | 120,535 | Ghia | 36,384 |
| 66H 2dr Sedan Ghia | 56,351 | Total | 369,936 |

## Serial Numbers

9F02Y100001

9 — Last digit of model year

F — Assembly plant (F-Dearborn, R-San Jose)

02 — Plate code for Mustang (02-2dr sedan, 03-3dr hatchback, 04-2dr Ghia, 05-3dr Ghia)

Y — Engine code

100001 — Consecutive unit number

### Location

Stamped on riveted plate on driver's side of dash, visible through the windshield; certification label attached on rear face of driver's door.

### Engine Codes

Y — 2.3 liter 2V 4 cyl 88 hp

W — 2.3 liter 2V 4 cyl 132 hp (Turbocharged)

Z — 2.8 liter 2V V-6 109 hp

T — 3.3 liter 1V 6 cyl 85 hp

F — 5.0 liter 2V V-8 140 hp

## 1979 Mustang Prices                                    Retail

| | |
|---|---|
| 2.3 liter 4 cyl Models | |
| 2dr Sedan | $4,494.00 |
| 3dr Sedan | 4,828.00 |
| 2dr Ghia | 5,064.00 |
| 3dr Ghia | 5,216.00 |
| 2.8 liter 6 cyl engine | 273.00 |
| 2.3 liter 4 cyl turbocharged | 542.00 |
| 3.3 liter 6 cyl | 241.00 |
| 5.0 liter, with Cobra Package | N/C |
| All others | 514.00 |
| SelectShift automatic | 307.00 |
| Accent Group, exterior | 72.00 |
| Accent Group, interior | |
| 2dr | 120.00 |
| 3dr | 108.00 |
| Air conditioner, SelectAire | 484.00 |
| Battery, heavy-duty | 18.00 |

| | |
|---|---:|
| Seatbelts, color-keyed deluxe | 20.00 |
| Bodyside protection, lower | 30.00 |
| Bracket, front license plate | N/C |
| Brakes, power front disc | 70.00 |
| Cobra Package | 1,173.00 |
| Cobra hood graphics | 78.00 |
| Console | 140.00 |
| Deflectors, mud & stone | 23.00 |
| Defroster, electric rear window | 84.00 |
| Emission system, Calif. | 76.00 |
| Emission system, high altitude | 33.00 |
| Exhaust, sport-tuned | 34.00 |
| Glass, tinted complete | 59.00 |
| Light Group, without flip-up open air roof | 37.00 |
| with open air roof | 25.00 |
| Lock Group, power | 99.00 |
| Mirror, lefthand remote-control | 18.00 |
| Mirrors, dual remote | 52.00 |
| Moldings, narrow vinyl insert bodyside | 39.00 |
| Moldings, rocker panel | 24.00 |
| Moldings, wide bodyside | 66.00 |
| Paint, metallic glow | 41.00 |
| Paint, lower Tu-tone | 78.00 |
| Protection Group, with front license plate bracket | 36.00 |
| without bracket | 33.00 |
| Radio flexibility option | 90.00 |
| Radio, AM | 84.00 |
| Radio, AM, digital clock | 131.00 |
| Radio, AM/FM monaural | 133.00 |
| Radio, AM/FM stereo | 188.00 |
| Radio, AM/FM stereo with cassette tape | 255.00 |
| Radio, AM/FM stereo with 8-track tape | 255.00 |
| Roof, flip-up open air | 199.00 |
| Roof, full vinyl | 102.00 |
| Seat, 4-way manual driver's | 35.00 |
| Sound system, premium | 67.00 |
| Speakers, dual rear seat | 42.00 |
| Speed control, fingertip, 2dr without Sport option | 116.00 |
| All others | 104.00 |
| Sport option | 175.00 |
| Steering, power variable ratio | 141.00 |
| Steering wheel, leather-wrapped sport | |
| 2dr without Sport option | 53.00 |
| All others | 41.00 |
| Steering wheel, tilt | |
| 2dr without Sport option | 81.00 |
| All others | 69.00 |
| Stripes, pin (bodyside and deck lid) | 30.00 |
| Suspension, handling | 33.00 |
| Trim, leather low-back bucket seat | 282.00 |
| Trim, cloth & vinyl seat | |
| Sedan | 20.00 |

| | |
|---|---:|
| Ghia | 42.00 |
| Trim, accent cloth and vinyl seat | 29.00 |
| Wheel covers, four turbine | |
|   3dr or with Sport option | 10.00 |
|   All others | 39.00 |
| Wheel covers, four wire | |
|   3dr or with Sport option | 70.00 |
|   Ghia | 60.00 |
|   All others | 99.00 |
| Wheels, four cast aluminum | |
|   3dr or with Sport option | 260.00 |
|   Ghia | 251.00 |
|   All others | 289.00 |
| Wheels, four forged metric aluminum | |
|   3dr or with Sport option | 269.00 |
|   Ghia | 259.00 |
|   All others | 298.00 |
| Wheels with trim rings, four styled steel | |
|   3dr or with Sport option | 65.00 |
|   Ghia | 55.00 |
|   All others | 94.00 |
| Windshield wipers, interval | 35.00 |
| Wiper/washer, rear window | 63.00 |
| Limited Production options | |
|   Floor mats, front (color-keyed) | 18.00 |
|   Heater, engine block immersion | 13.00 |
|   Light, luggage compartment | 5.00 |
|   Tinted glass, windshield | 25.00 |
| Tires, Models having four B78x13 bias ply BSW as standard equipment, extra charge for: | |
|   B78x13 bias WSW | 43.00 |
|   C78x13 bias BSW | 25.00 |
|   C78x13 bias WSW | 69.00 |
|   B78x14 bias WSW | 66.00 |
|   C78x14 bias BSW | 48.00 |
|   BR78x14 BSW | 124.00 |
|   BR78x14 WSW | 167.00 |
|   CR78x14 WSW | 192.00 |
|   CR78x14 RWL | 209.00 |
|   TRX 190/65Rx390 BSW Michelin* | 241.00 |
| Models having four BR78x14 BSW tires as standard equipment, extra charge for: | |
|   BR78x14 WSW | 43.00 |
|   CR78x14 WSW | 69.00 |
|   CR78x14 RWL | 86.00 |
|   TRX 190/65Rx390 BSW Michelin* | 117.00 |
|     *Requires forged metric aluminum wheels | |

| 1979 Exterior Colors | Code | 1979 Exterior Colors | Code |
|---|---|---|---|
| Black | 1C | Red Glow | 2H |
| Silver Metallic | 1G | Bright Red | 2P |

## 1979 Exterior Colors

| Colors | Code |
|---|---|
| Light Medium Blue | 3F |
| Medium Blue Glow | 3H |
| Bright Blue | 3J |
| Dark Jade Metallic | 46 |
| Medium Chestnut Metallic | 5M |
| Medium Vaquero Gold | 5W |
| Bright Yellow | 64 |
| Light Chamois | 83 |
| Tangerine | 85 |
| Medium Grey Metallic | 1P |
| Polar White | 9D |

## Tu-tone Exterior Color Combinations

| Body color/accent color | Code |
|---|---|
| All/Black | /1C |

## Tu-tone Exterior Color Combinations

| | Code |
|---|---|
| Silver Metallic/ Medium Grey Metallic | 1G/1P |
| Light Medium Blue/ Bright Blue | 3F/3J |

## 1979 Interior Trim

| Trim | Code |
|---|---|
| Black | A |
| Red | D |
| Wedgewood Blue | B |
| Chamois | T |
| White/Red | N |
| White/Black | W |
| White/Chamois | 2 |
| White/Blue | Q |

## 1979 Mustang Facts

The Mustang went through its third major change in 1979. Retaining the basic dimensions of the Mustang II, the Mustang's wheelbase was increased to 100.4 inches (from 96.2), which translated into a roomier passenger compartment. The 1979 Mustang was a totally new design with no styling references to the original Mustang or Mustang II. Two body styles were available, a two-door sedan and the three-door hatchback.

Sharing many components from the Fairmont/Zephyr platform, the 1979 Mustang was the first Mustang to use a strut-type front suspension—with a slight variation. Whereas the typical strut suspension has the front coil spring mounted around the strut, in the Mustang the coil spring was located between the lower control arm and chassis. The rear 6.75 inch axle was located by a four-bar link arrangement as the Mustang used coil springs in the rear for the first time. Steering was a carryover and brakes were front discs/rear drums.

Engine availability was similar to the Mustang II's. The 2.3 liter four-cylinder was standard equipment, the German made 2.8 liter V-6 optional and the 5.0 liter V-8 was still available as the only V-8 option. For the first time, the 302 was fitted with a single-belt (serpentine) accessory drive system.

An unreliable turbocharged version of the 2.3 liter four-cylinder was optional as well, generating 132 hp. A lot of hoopla was made about this engine, but Ford was forced to withdraw it for a variety of mechanical ills after the 1980 model year.

The old 200 ci inline six (3.3L) replaced the German V-6 midway through the model year.

An effort was made to improve the Mustang's handling. The optional handling suspension came with a 0.50 inch rear stabilizer bar (0.56 inch with the 2.8 V-6). The 0.50 inch bar was also standard with the 302 ci engine. More significant was the suspension package that was included when the Michelin 190/65R 390 TRX tires and TR 390 forged aluminum wheels were ordered. Shocks, springs and stabilizer bars were tuned to the TRX wheels/tires to provide excellent handling, especially on smooth surfaces. As good as the tires were, the 302's torque could easily overwhelm them resulting in wheel spin and lots of wheel hop. The wheel hop problem, due more to the rear suspension's design, wasn't really effectively solved until 1984 with the introduction of the Quadra-Shock rear on the SVO and later on the 5.0L GTs.

The Ghia model still stressed luxury with usual interior upgrades and Ghia emblems. The performance-oriented option was the Cobra package, available only on the three-door hatchback. Standard engine was the 2.3L Turbocharged four-cylinder, with the 5.0L V-8 optional, and the Michelin TRX wheels/tires combination.

The most significant 1979 Mustang was the 1979½ Pace Car. As in 1964, Mustang was chosen for use in the 1979 Indy 500. Unlike in 1964, 11,000 pace car replicas were built. Engine availability was limited to the 302 or the Turbo four-cylinder. All pace cars had the same pewter/black paint treatment highlighted with orange and red tape stripes. Pace car lettering decals were dealer or customer installed. Other features were a rear spoiler, front air dam with integral foglamps, pop-up sunroof, rear facing non-functional hood scoop, TRX wheels and tires, and the interior sported Recaro seats finished in a unique pattern.

*1979 Pace Car* Ford Motor Co.

# Chapter 16

# 1980 Mustang

## Production Figures

| | | | |
|---|---|---|---|
| 66B 2dr Sedan | 128,893 | 61R 3dr Hatchback | |
| 66H 2dr Sedan Ghia | 23,647 | Sport | 98,497 |
| 61H 3dr Hatchback | | Total | 271,322 |
| Ghia | 20,285 | | |

## Serial Numbers

0F02A100001

0 — Last digit of model year

F — Assembly plant (F-Dearborn, R-San Jose)

02 — Plate code for Mustang (02-2dr sedan, 03-3dr hatchback, 04-2dr Ghia, 05-3dr Ghia)

A — Engine code

100001 — Consecutive unit number

### Location

Stamped on riveted plate on driver's side of dash, visible through the windshield; certification label attached on rear face of driver's door.

### Engine Codes

A — 2.3 liter 2V 4 cyl 88 hp(MT), 90 hp (AT)

W — 2.3 liter 2V 4 cyl (Turbocharged)

B — 3.3 liter 1V 6 cyl 91 hp(MT), 94 hp(AT)

D — 4.2 liter 2V V-8 119 hp

## 1980 Mustang Prices

| | Retail |
|---|---|
| 2.3 liter 4 cyl Models | |
| 2dr Sedan | $5,338.00 |
| 3dr Sedan | 5,616.00 |
| 2dr Ghia | 5,823.00 |
| 3dr Ghia | 5,935.00 |
| 3.3 liter (200 cid) 6 cyl | 256.00 |
| 4.2 liter (255 cid) 8 cyl, with Cobra Package | (144.00) |
| All others | 338.00 |
| 2.3 liter 4 cyl Turbocharged | 481.00 |
| SelectShift automatic transmission | 340.00 |
| 5-speed manual overdrive | 156.00 |
| Axle, optional ratio | 18.00 |
| Accent Group, exterior | 63.00 |
| Accent Group, interior, 2dr sedan | 134.00 |
| 3dr sedan | 120.00 |
| Air conditioner, SelectAire | 538.00 |
| Battery, heavy-duty | 20.00 |
| Seatbelts, color-keyed deluxe | 23.00 |

| | |
|---|---:|
| Bodyside protection, lower | 34.00 |
| Bracket, front license plate | N/C |
| Brakes, power front disc | 78.00 |
| Cargo area cover | 44.00 |
| Cobra Package | 1,482.00 |
| Cobra hood graphics | 88.00 |
| Console | 166.00 |
| Deflectors, mud & stone | 25.00 |
| Defroster, electric rear window | 96.00 |
| Emission system, Calif. | 253.00 |
| Emission system, high altitude | 36.00 |
| Exhaust system, sport-tuned | |
|     With 2.3 liter turbocharged and automatic | N/C |
|     With 4.2 liter engine | 38.00 |
| Glass, tinted complete | 65.00 |
| Heater, engine block immersion | 15.00 |
| Hood scoop | 31.00 |
| Light Group | 41.00 |
| Lock Group, power | 113.00 |
| Louvers, liftgate | 141.00 |
| Luggage carrier, roof-mounted | 86.00 |
| Mirror, lefthand remote-control | 19.00 |
| Mirrors, dual remote-control (black) | 58.00 |
| Moldings, rocker panel | 30.00 |
| Moldings, vinyl insert bodyside (narrow) | 43.00 |
| Moldings, vinyl insert bodyside (wide) | 74.00 |
| Paint, metallic glow | 46.00 |
| Paint treatment, lower Tu-tone | 88.00 |
| Premium sound system | 94.00 |
| Protection Group, appearance | |
|     With front license plate bracket | 41.00 |
|     Without bracket | 38.00 |
| Radio, AM delete | (93.00) |
| Radio, AM/FM monaural | 53.00 |
| Radio, AM/FM stereo | 90.00 |
| Radio, AM/FM stereo with cassette tape | 179.00 |
| Radio, AM/FM stereo with 8-track tape | 166.00 |
| Radio flexibility option | 63.00 |
| Roof, carriage | 625.00 |
| Roof, flip-up open air, Ghia or w/Light Group | 204.00 |
|     All others | 219.00 |
| Roof, full vinyl | 118.00 |
| Seats, Recaro high-back buckets | 531.00 |
| Seat, 4-way manual driver's | 38.00 |
| Speakers, dual rear seat | 38.00 |
| Speed control, fingertip,2dr without Sport option | 129.00 |
|     All others | 116.00 |
| Sport option, with Carriage Roof | 168.00 |
|     without Carriage Roof | 186.00 |
| Steering, power | 160.00 |
| Steering wheel, leather-wrapped | |
|     2dr without Sport option | 56.00 |

| | |
|---|---:|
| All others | 44.00 |
| Steering wheel, tilt | |
| 2dr without Sport option | 90.00 |
| All others | 78.00 |
| Stripes, accent tape | |
| with Exterior Accent Group | 19.00 |
| without Accent Group | 53.00 |
| Stripes, pin (bodyside and deck lid) | 34.00 |
| Suspension, handling | 35.00 |
| Trim, accent cloth and vinyl seat | 30.00 |
| Trim, leather low-back bucket seat | 349.00 |
| Trim, cloth and vinyl bucket seat, Sedans | 21.00 |
| Ghia | 46.00 |
| Wheel covers, four turbine | |
| 3dr or with Sport option | 10.00 |
| All others | 43.00 |
| Wheel covers, four wire | |
| 3dr or with Sport option | 89.00 |
| Ghia | 79.00 |
| All others | 121.00 |
| Wheels, four cast aluminum | |
| 3dr or with Sport option | 289.00 |
| Ghia | 279.00 |
| All others | 321.00 |
| Wheels, four forged metric aluminum | |
| 3dr or with Sport option | 323.00 |
| Ghia models | 313.00 |
| All others | 355.00 |
| Wheels with trim rings, four styled steel | |
| 3dr or with Sport option | 71.00 |
| Ghia | 61.00 |
| All others | 104.00 |
| Windshield wipers, interval | 39.00 |
| Wiper/washer, rear window | 79.00 |
| Limited Production options | |
| Floor mats, front color-keyed | 19.00 |
| Light, luggage compartment | 5.00 |
| Tinted glass, windshield | 29.00 |
| Tires, models having four 185/80Rx13 radial ply BSW as standard equipment, extra charge for four: | |
| P185/80Rx13 WSW | 50.00 |
| P175/75Rx14 BSW | 25.00 |
| P175/75Rx14 WSW | 75.00 |
| P185/75Rx14 BSW | 50.00 |
| P185/75Rx14 WSW | 100.00 |
| P185/75Rx14 RWL | 117.00 |
| TRX 190/65Rx390 BSW* | 150.00 |
| Models having four P175/75Rx14 Radial ply BSW as standard equipment, extra charge for four: | |
| P175/75Rx14 WSW | 50.00 |
| P185/75Rx14 BSW | 25.00 |
| P185/75Rx14 WSW | 75.00 |

| | |
|---|---|
| P185/75Rx14 RWL | 92.00 |
| TRX 190/65Rx390 BSW* | 125.00 |

*Require forged metric aluminum wheels

## 1980 Exterior Colors

| Colors | Code |
|---|---|
| Black | 1C |
| Bright Blue | 3J |
| Bright Yellow | 6N |
| Polar White | 9D |
| Silver Metallic | 1G |
| Medium Grey Metallic | 1P |
| Bright Caramel | 5T |
| Dark Chamois Metallic | 8A |
| Bright Bittersweet | 2G |
| Light Medium Blue | 3F |
| Dark Cordovan Metallic | 8N |
| Bright Red | 27 |
| Bittersweet Glow | 8D |
| Medium Blue Glow | 3H |
| Chamois Glow | 8W |

## Tu-tone Exterior Color Combinations

| | Code |
|---|---|
| Dark Chamois Metallic/Chamois Glow | 8A/8W |
| Polar White/Bright Yellow | 9D/6N |
| Light Medium Blue/Bright Blue | 3F/3J |
| Bright Bittersweet/Dark Cordovan Metallic | 2G/8N |
| Polar White/Bittersweet Glow | 9D/8D |
| Silver Metallic/Dark Cordovan Metallic | 1G/8N |
| Chamois Glow/Dark Chamois Metallic | 8W/8A |

## Tu-tone Exterior Color Combinations

| Upper color/lower color | Code |
|---|---|
| Silver Metallic/Medium Grey Metallic | 1G/1P |
| Dark Cordovan Metallic/Bittersweet Glow | 8N/8D |
| Bittersweet Glow/Dark Cordovan Metallic | 8D/8N |

## 1980 Interior Trim

| Trim | Code |
|---|---|
| Black | A |
| Wedgewood Blue | B |
| Bittersweet | C |
| Red | D |
| White/Red | N |
| White/Blue | Q |
| Caramel | T |
| White/Black | W |
| Vaquero | Z |
| White/Caramel | 2 |
| White/Vaquero | 9 |

## 1980 Mustang Facts

Very little was done in terms of styling in 1980. The biggest change was the downsizing of the 302 ci V-8 to an anemic 255 ci, putting out a paltry 119 hp. The cubic inch reduction was achieved by decreasing the bore from 4.00 inches to 3.68 inches. The 255 was only available with the automatic transmission.

Otherwise, engine choice remained the same—2.3L standard equipment with the 3.3L six and Turbocharged 2.3 four optional. You could also get the 2.3 Turbo with an automatic transmission.

The hot-dog Cobra model got the pace car's front and rear spoilers, rear opening (simulated) hood scoop, standard 2.3 Turbo engine (the 255 V-8 was optional), TRX wheels and tires, the sport-tuned exhaust system, dual black remote-control mirrors and the blacked-out treatment. The blacked-out treatment was extended to the interior as the dash panel got black engine-turned appliques.

The Recaro seats, first seen on the 1979½ Pace Car, were now optional on all Mustangs. They were a fairly expensive option at $531.00.

There were few changes with the luxury Ghia model, which got a restyled steering wheel. Emulating the convertible look was the Carriage Roof option available only on the two-door models.

The Sport option was still available on the three-door, consisting of styled steel wheels with trim rings, black rocker panel and window moldings, and bodyside moldings.

For the first time, the Mustang came equipped with halogen headlights, a maintenance-free battery and the P-metric radial tires.

New on the option list was the roof-mounted luggage carrier and cargo cover for the hatchbacks.

*1980 three-door Cobra* Ford Motor Co.

# Chapter 17

# 1981 Mustang

## Production Figures

| | | | |
|---|---|---|---|
| 66B 2dr Sedan | 77,458 | 61H 3dr Hatchback | |
| 66H 2dr Sedan Ghia | 13,422 | Ghia | 14,273 |
| 61R 3dr Hatchback | 77,399 | Total | 182,552 |

## Serial Numbers

1FABP10A6BF000001

1FA — Ford Motor Co.

B — Restraint system (B-active belts)

P — Passenger car

10 — Body code (10/14-2dr sedan, 15-3dr, 12-2dr Ghia, 13-3dr Ghia)

A — Engine code

6 — Check digit which varies

B — Year (B-1981)

F — Plant (F-Dearborn)

000001 — Consecutive unit number

### Location

Stamped on riveted plate on driver's side of dash, visible through the windshield; certification label attached on rear face of driver's door.

### Engine Codes

A — 2.3 liter 2V 4 cyl 88 hp

B — 3.3 liter 1V 6 cyl 94 hp

D — 4.2 liter 2V V-8, 120 hp

## 1981 Mustang Prices      Retail

| | |
|---|---|
| 2dr Sedan, P10/14H | $5,897.00 |
| 2dr Sedan, P10 | 6,363.00 |
| 3dr Sedan, P15 | 6,566.00 |
| 3dr Ghia, P12 | 6,786.00 |
| 3dr Ghia, P13 | 6,901.00 |
| 3.3L 6 cyl engine | 213.00 |
| 4.2L 8 cyl engine | 263.00 |
| 5-speed manual overdrive | 183.00 |
| SelectShift automatic | 370.00 |
| Traction-Lok axle | 71.00 |
| Tires, extra charge for four: | |
|     P175/75Rx14 WSW | 59.00 |
|     P185x75Rx14 BSW | 28.00 |
|     P185x75Rx14 WSW | 86.00 |
|     P185x75Rx14 RWL | 107.00 |
|     190/65Rx390 TRX, requires forged metric wheels | 135.00 |
| Air conditioner, SelectAire | 600.00 |

| | |
|---|---:|
| Battery, heavy-duty | 22.00 |
| Seatbelts, color-keyed deluxe | 24.00 |
| Bodyside protection lower | 39.00 |
| Bracket, front license plate | N/C |
| Brakes, power front disc | 87.00 |
| Cargo area cover | 48.00 |
| Cobra option | 1,075.00 |
| Cobra hood graphics | 95.00 |
| Cobra tape treatment, delete | (65.00) |
| Console | 178.00 |
| Deflectors, mud & stone | 27.00 |
| Defroster, rear window electric | 115.00 |
| Floor mats, front color-keyed | 20.00 |
| Glass, tinted complete | 82.00 |
| Hood scoop | 35.00 |
| Interior Accent Group, 2dr | 159.00 |
|    3dr | 145.00 |
| Light Group | 45.00 |
| Lock Group, power | 129.00 |
| Louvers, liftgate | 154.00 |
| Luggage carrier, roof-mounted | 99.00 |
| Mirror, lefthand remote-control | 22.00 |
| Mirrors, dual remote-control, black | 61.00 |
| Moldings, rocker panel, black | 30.00 |
| Paint treatment, lower Tu-tone | 96.00 |
| Paint, Special Tu-tone | |
|    Ghia | 128.00 |
|    All others | 165.00 |
| Protection Group, appearance | 44.00 |
| Radio, AM/FM monaural | 51.00 |
| Radio, AM/FM stereo | 88.00 |
| Radio, AM with dual rear seat speakers | |
|    (price for speakers) | 39.00 |
| Radio, AM/FM monaural with dual rear seat speakers | |
|    (price for speakers) | 39.00 |
| Radio, AM/FM stereo with cassette tape | 174.00 |
| Radio, AM/FM stereo with 8–track tape | 162.00 |
| Radio flexibility option | 65.00 |
| Radio flexibility option with dual rear seat speakers | |
|    (price for speakers) | 39.00 |
| Radio, AM delete | (61.00) |
| Sound system, premium | 98.00 |
| Roof, flip-up open air | |
|    Ghia or with Light Group | 227.00 |
|    All others | 241.00 |
| Roof, "T" | 916.00 |
| Speed control, fingertip | 145.00 |
| Sport option, with Carriage Roof | 62.00 |
|    without Carriage Roof | 82.00 |
| Steering, power | 176.00 |
| Steering wheel, leather-wrapped | |
|    2dr without Sport option | 63.00 |

| | |
|---|---:|
| All others | 51.00 |
| Steering wheel, tilt | |
| 2dr without Sport option | 100.00 |
| All others | 88.00 |
| Stripes, accent tape | 57.00 |
| Stripes, pin | 37.00 |
| Suspension, handling | 46.00 |
| Wheel covers, four turbine | 46.00 |
| Wheel covers, four wire | |
| Ghia | 85.00 |
| All others | 132.00 |
| Wheels, four cast aluminum | |
| Ghia | 323.00 |
| All others | 370.00 |
| Wheels, four forged metric aluminum | |
| Ghia | 361.00 |
| All others | 407.00 |
| Wheels with trim rings, four styled steel | |
| Ghia | 67.00 |
| All others | 113.00 |
| Windows, power side | 152.00 |
| Windshield wipers, interval | 44.00 |
| Wiper/washer, rear window | 94.00 |
| Emission system, Calif. | 46.00 |
| Emission system, high altitude | 40.00 |
| Exterior glow paint | 50.00 |
| Recaro high-back bucket seats | 776.00 |
| Accent cloth & vinyl seat trim | 34.00 |
| Cloth & vinyl bucket seat trim | |
| Sedans | 23.00 |
| Ghia | 51.00 |
| Leather low-back bucket seat trim | 380.00 |
| Full vinyl roof | 127.00 |
| Carriage roof | 683.00 |
| Limited Production options | |
| Floor mats, front carpet (color-keyed) | 20.00 |
| Glass, tinted, windshield only | 29.00 |
| Heater, engine block immersion | 16.00 |
| Light, luggage compartment | 6.00 |

## 1981 Exterior Colors

| Colors | Code | Colors | Code |
|---|---|---|---|
| Black | 1C | Polar White | 9D |
| Light Pewter Metallic | 1T | Medium Pewter Metallic | 17 |
| Bright Bittersweet | 2G | Red | 24 |
| Midnight Blue Metallic | 3L | Bright Red | 27 |
| Dark Brown Metallic | 5Q | Pastel Chamois | 86 |
| Bright Yellow | 6N | Medium Blue Glow | 3H |
| Dark Cordovan Metallic | 8N | Bittersweet Glow | 8D |

## Tu-tone Exterior Color Combinations

| Upper color/lower color | Code |
|---|---|
| Light Pewter Metallic/Black | 1T/1C |
| Medium Pewter Metallic/Black | 17/1C |
| Bright Bittersweet/Black | 2G/1C |
| Red/Black | 24/1C |
| Bright Red/Black | 27/1C |
| Bright Yellow/Black | 6N/1C |
| Bittersweet Glow/Black | 8D/1C |
| Dark Cordovan Metallic/Black | 8N/1C |
| Pastel Chamois/Black | 86/1C |
| Polar White/Black | 9D/1C |

## Tu-tone Exterior Color Combinations

| Upper color/lower color | Code |
|---|---|
| Medium Pewter Metallic/Light Pewter Metallic | 17/1T |
| Red/Polar White | 24/9D |
| Polar White/Bittersweet Glow | 9D/8D |

## 1981 Interior Trim

| Trim | Code |
|---|---|
| Black | A |
| Wedgewood Blue | B |
| Red | D |
| Caramel | T |
| Pewter | P |
| Vaquero | Z |

## 1981 Mustang Facts

Although early factory literature listed the 2.3L Turbo as an option, the engine was in fact dropped for reliability problems. Otherwise engine availability was the same as in 1980.

New options included a five-speed manual overdrive transmission (introduced during 1980), the Traction-Lok differential for the rear, rear window louvers for the hatchback and the T-roof, this time optional on both Mustang body styles.

Power windows were optional for the first time, too.

1981 was the last year of the Cobra option package, which continued basically unchanged from 1980.

*1981 two-door* Ford Motor Co.

# Chapter 18

# 1982 Mustang

## Production Figures

| | | | |
|---|---|---|---|
| 66B 2dr Sedan | 45,316 | 61H 3dr Hatchback | |
| 66H 2dr Sedan GLX | 5,828 | GLX | 9,926 |
| 61B 3dr Hatchback | 69,348 | Total | 130,418 |

## Serial Numbers

1FABP10A6CF000001

1FA — Ford Motor Co.

B — Restraint system (B-active belts)

P — Passenger car

10 — Body code (10-2dr L/GL, 16-3dr GL/GT, 12-2dr GLX, 13-3dr GLX)

A — Engine code

6 — Check digit which varies

C — Year (C-1982)

F — Plant (F-Dearborn)

000001 — Consecutive unit number

**Location**

Stamped on riveted plate on driver's side of dash, visible through the windshield; certification label attached on rear face of driver's door.

**Engine Codes**

A — 2.3 liter 2V 4 cyl 88 hp

B — 3.3 liter 1V 6 cyl 94 hp

D — 4.2 liter 2V V-8 120 hp

F — 5.0 liter 2V V-8 157 hp

## 1982 Mustang Prices

| | Retail |
|---|---|
| 2dr L Sedan, P10 | $6,345.00 |
| 2dr GL Sedan, P10 | 6,844.00 |
| 3dr GL Sedan, P16 | 6,979.00 |
| 2dr GLX Sedan, P12 | 6,980.00 |
| 3dr GLX Sedan, P13 | 7,101.00 |
| 3dr GT Sedan, P16 | 8,397.00 |
| 3.3L 6 cyl engine | 213.00 |
| 4.2L 8 cyl engine | |
| GL | (57.00) |
| All others | 283.00 |
| 5.0L 8 cyl engine (std. on GT) | |
| Use with TR Performance Package | 494.00 |
| All others | 544.00 |
| 5-speed manual overdrive | 196.00 |
| SelectShift automatic | 411.00 |
| Optional ratio | N/C |

| | |
|---|---:|
| Traction-Lok axle | 76.00 |
| Tires, extra charge for four (except GT): | |
|     P175/75Rx14 WSW | 72.00 |
|     P185/75Rx14 BSW | 36.00 |
|     P185/75Rx14 WSW | 108.00 |
|     P185/75Rx14 RWL | 128.00 |
| GT, extra charge for four: | |
|     P185/75Rx14 WSW | 72.00 |
|     P185/75Rx14 RWL | 91.00 |
| Air conditioner, SelectAire | 688.00 |
| Battery, heavy-duty | 24.00 |
| Bodyside protection, lower | 41.00 |
| Bracket, front license plate | N/C |
| Brakes, power front disc | 93.00 |
| Cargo area cover | 51.00 |
| Console | 191.00 |
| Defroster, rear window electric | 124.00 |
| Glass, tinted complete | 88.00 |
| Hood scoop | 38.00 |
| Light Group | 49.00 |
| Lock Group, power | 139.00 |
| Louvers, liftgate | 165.00 |
| Mirror, righthand remote-control | 41.00 |
| Moldings, rocker panel, black | 33.00 |
| Paint treatment, lower Tu-tone | 116.00 |
| Paint, Special Tu-tone | |
|     GL & GLX | 150.00 |
|     L | 189.00 |
| Protection Group, appearance | 48.00 |
| Radio, AM/FM monaural | 76.00 |
| Radio, AM with dual rear seat speakers | |
|     (price for speakers) | 39.00 |
| Radio, AM/FM monaural with dual rear seat speakers | |
|     (price for speakers) | 39.00 |
| Radio, AM/FM stereo with cassette tape | 184.00 |
| Radio, AM/FM stereo with 8-track tape | 184.00 |
| AM radio credit option | (61.00) |
| Sound system, premium | 117.00 |
| Roof, flip-up open air | 276.00 |
| Roof, "T" | 1,021.00 |
| Speed control, fingertip | 155.00 |
| Steering, power | 202.00 |
| Steering wheel, leather-wrapped | 55.00 |
| Steering wheel, tilt | 95.00 |
| Stripes, accent tape | 62.00 |
| Suspension, handling | 50.00 |
| TR Performance Suspension Package | |
|     L | 589.00 |
|     GL & GLX | 539.00 |
|     GT | 111.00 |
| Wheel covers, four wire | |
|     L | 148.00 |

| | |
|---|---|
| GL & GLX | 98.00 |
| Wheels, four cast aluminum | |
| L | 404.00 |
| GL & GLX | 354.00 |
| Wheels with trim rings, four styled steel | |
| L | 128.00 |
| GL & GLX | 78.00 |
| Windows, power side | 165.00 |
| Windshield wipers, interval | 48.00 |
| Wiper/washer, rear window | 101.00 |
| Emission system, Calif. | 46.00 |
| Emission system, high altitude | N/C |
| Metallic glow paint | 54.00 |
| Recaro high-back bucket seats | 834.00 |
| Cloth & vinyl seat trim | |
| L | 29.00 |
| GL | 40.00 |
| GLX & GT | 57.00 |
| Leather, low bucket seat trim | 415.00 |
| Full vinyl roof | 149.00 |
| Carriage roof | 746.00 |
| Limited Production options | |
| Floor mats, front carpet, color-keyed | 22.00 |
| Glass, tinted, windshield only | 32.00 |
| Heater, engine block, immersion | 17.00 |
| Light, luggage compartment | 7.00 |

## 1982 Exterior Colors

| Colors | Code |
|---|---|
| Black | 1C |
| Silver Metallic | 1G |
| Medium Grey Metallic | 1P |
| Red | 24 |
| Bright Red | 27 |
| Dark Blue Metallic | 3D |
| Medium Vanilla | 6Y |
| Pastel Vanilla | 6Z |
| Medium Yellow | 61 |
| Dark Curry Brown Metallic | 69 |
| Dark Cordovan Metallic | 8N |
| Polar White | 9D |
| Medium Blue Glow | 3H |
| Bittersweet Glow | 8D |

## Tu-tone Exterior Color Combinations

| Upper color/lower color | Code |
|---|---|
| Medium Grey Metallic/ Silver Metallic | 1P/1G |

## Tu-tone Exterior Color Combinations

| Upper color/lower color | Code |
|---|---|
| Dark Blue Metallic/ Medium Blue Glow | 3D/3H |
| Medium Vanilla/ Pastel Vanilla | 6Y/6Z |
| Dark Cordovan Metallic/ Bittersweet Glow | 8N/8D |
| Silver Metallic/Black | 1G/1C |
| Medium Grey Metallic/ Black | 1P/1C |
| Red/Black | 24/1C |
| Bright Red/Black | 27/1C |
| Dark Blue Metallic/ Black | 3D/1C |
| Medium Blue Glow/ Black | 3H/1C |
| Medium Vanilla/Black | 6Y/1C |
| Pastel Vanilla/Black | 6Z/1C |
| Medium Yellow/Black | 61/1C |
| Dark Cordovan Metallic/Black | 8N/1C |

| Tu-tone Exterior Color Combinations | | 1982 Interior Trim | Code |
|---|---|---|---|
| Upper color/lower | | Black | A |
| color | Code | Wedgewood Blue | B |
| Bittersweet Glow/ | | Red | D |
| Black | 8D/1C | Vaquero | Z |
| Polar White/Black | 9D/1C | White/Vaquero | 9 |
| | | Opal/Red | N |
| | | French Vanilla | V |
| | | Opal/Black | W |
| | | Opal/Vaquero | 9 |

## 1982 Mustang Facts

The most significant change of 1982 was the reintroduction of the Mustang GT and the 302 ci V-8, dubbed the 5.0L H.O. Although the 5.0L engine could be had on any Mustang, the Mustang GT model included the engine as standard equipment along with a host of other options.

The resurrected 5.0L came with stouter internal components such as a double roller timing chain, and a higher lift cam (as compared to the 1979 version).

Mandatory options with the 5.0 included the four-speed manual overdrive, 3.08 Traction-Lok rear, power brakes, power steering and the handling suspension which included traction bars for the 5.0. Fourteen-inch cast aluminum wheels with P185/75R14 tires were standard; the TRX wheels/tires/suspension was optional.

The GT also came with a slightly redesigned grille, forward facing non-functional hood scoop and the pace car air dam and rear spoiler. Color choice was limited to three—Red, Black or Metallic Silver with red or black interiors. Extensive use of black paint in the interior and blacked-out treatment on the exterior served to enhance the Mustang's new-found performance image.

All Ford engines beginning in 1982 were painted a light gray.

*1982 three-door GT*

# Chapter 19

# 1983 Mustang

## Production Figures

| | | | |
|---|---|---|---|
| 66B 2dr Sedan | 33,201 | 61B 3dr Hatchback | 64,234 |
| 66B 2dr Convertible | 23,438 | Total | 120,873 |

## Serial Numbers

1FABP26A6DF000001

1FA — Ford Motor Co.

B — Restraint system (B-active belts)

P — Passenger car

26 — Body code (26-2dr sedan, 27-2dr convertible, 28-3dr hatchback)

A — Engine code

6 — Check digit which varies

D — Year (D-1983)

F — Assembly plant (F-Dearborn)

000001 — Consecutive unit number

### Location

Stamped on plate riveted on driver's side of dash, visible through the windshield; certification label attached on rear face of driver's door.

### Engine Codes

A — 2.3L 1V 4 cyl 88 hp

T — 2.3L EFI 4 cyl 145 hp (Turbo GT)

3 — 3.8L 2V V-6 112 hp

M — 5.0L 4V V-8 175 hp (HO)

## 1983 Mustang Prices

| | Retail |
|---|---|
| 2dr L Sedan, P26 | $6,727.00 |
| 2dr GL Sedan, P26/60C | 7,264.00 |
| 3dr GL Sedan, P28/60C | 7,439.00 |
| 2dr GLX Sedan, P26/602 | 7,398.00 |
| 2dr GLX Convertible, P27/602 | 12,467.00 |
| 3dr GLX Sedan, P28/602 | 7,557.00 |
| 3dr GT Sedan, P28/932 | 9,449.00 |
| 3dr Turbo GT, P28/932 | 9,714.00 |
| 2dr GT Convertible, P27/932 | 13,479.00 |
| 3.8L 6 cyl (std. GLX Convertible) | 309.00 |
| 5.0L 4V HO 8 cyl package, 5-speed transmission (std. on GT, except Turbo GT) | |
|     GLX Convertible | 719.00 |
|     All others | 1,467.00 |
| 5-speed manual overdrive (std. GT & 5.0L) | 124.00 |
| SelectShift automatic (std. GLX Convertible) | 439.00 |

| | |
|---|---|
| 4-speed manual credit | |
|     (for GT or with 5.0L, NA Turbo GT) | (124.00) |
| Optional axle ratio | N/C |
| Traction-Lok axle | 95.00 |
| Tires, extra charge for four (except GT & models with 5.0L): | |
|     P185/75Rx14 WSW | 72.00 |
|     P195/75Rx14 WSW | 108.00 |
|     P205/70HRx14 BSW | 224.00 |
|     Michelin TRX P220/55R 390 BSW | 551.00 |
|     GT (credit) | (27.00) |
|     Models with 5.0L | 327.00 |
| Air conditioner, SelectAire | 737.00 |
| Battery, heavy-duty | 26.00 |
| Bodyside protection, lower | 41.00 |
| Bracket, front license plate | N/C |
| Brakes, power front disc | 93.00 |
| Console | 191.00 |
| Defroster, rear window electric | 135.00 |
| Glass, tinted complete | 105.00 |
| Light Group | 55.00 |
| Lock Group, power | 172.00 |
| Louvers, liftgate | 171.00 |
| Mirror, righthand remote-control | 44.00 |
| Moldings, rocker panel, black | 39.00 |
| Paint treatment, lower Tu-tone | 116.00 |
| Paint, special Tu-tone | |
|     GL & GLX | 150.00 |
|     L | 189.00 |
| Protection Group, appearance | 39.00 |
| Radio, AM/FM monaural | 82.00 |
| Radio, AM/FM stereo | 109.00 |
| Radio, AM/FM stereo with cassette tape | 199.00 |
| Radio, AM/FM stereo with 8-track tape | 199.00 |
| AM radio credit option | (61.00) |
| Sound system, premium | 117.00 |
| Roof, flip-up open air | 310.00 |
| Roof, "T" | 1,074.00 |
| Speed control, fingertip | 170.00 |
| Steering, power | 202.00 |
| Steering wheel, leather-wrapped | 59.00 |
| Steering wheel, tilt | 105.00 |
| Suspension package, handling | 252.00 |
| Wheel covers, four turbine | N/C |
| Wheel covers, four wire | |
|     L | 148.00 |
|     GL & GLX | 98.00 |
| Wheels, four cast aluminum | |
|     L | 404.00 |
|     GL & GLX | 354.00 |
| Wheels with trim rings, four styled steel | |
|     L | 128.00 |

| GL & GLX | 78.00 |
|---|---|
| Windows, power front | 193.00 |
| Windshield wipers, interval | 49.00 |
| Delete standard accent stripe | N/C |
| Emissions system, Calif. | 76.00 |
| Emissions system, high altitude | N/C |
| Metallic glow paint | 54.00 |
| Cloth sports performance seats | 196.00 |
| Cloth & vinyl seat trim | |
|    L | 29.00 |
|    GL | 40.00 |
|    GLX and GT | 57.00 |
| Leather low-back bucket seat trim | 415.00 |
| Limited Production options | |
|    Floor mats, front carpet, color-keyed | 22.00 |
|    Glass, tinted, windshield only | 38.00 |
|    Heater, engine block immersion | 17.00 |

| 1983 Exterior Colors | Code |
|---|---|
| Black | 1C |
| Polar White | 9D |
| Silver Metallic | 1G |
| Medium Charcoal Metallic | 1B |
| Red | 24 |
| Bright Red | 27 |
| Dark Academy Blue Metallic | 3D |
| Dark Walnut Metallic | 5U |
| Light Desert Tan | 8Q |
| Medium Yellow | 61 |
| Midnight Blue Metallic | 3L |
| Light Academy Blue Glow | 38 |

| 1983 Exterior Colors | Code |
|---|---|
| Desert Tan Glow | 9N |
| Bright Bittersweet | 2G |

| 1983 Interior Trim | Code |
|---|---|
| Black | A |
| Cadet Blue | B |
| Red | D |
| Walnut | E |
| Opal/Red | N |
| Opal/Blue | Q |
| Opal/Black | W |
| Opal/Walnut | Z |

## 1983 Mustang Facts

The 1983 Mustang featured a new front end treatment and new rear taillight lenses. A third body style, the convertible in GL or GT forms, was added. Mechanically, the Mustang was the focus of considerable improvement. In spite of all this, the 1983 Mustang had the distinction of being the lowest-selling up to that time.

Model configuration was similar to 1982. The base Mustang was the L two-door. The upgraded GL was available in two-door, three-door and convertible while the GLX could be had in two- or three-door versions. The 3dr GT was joined by the three-door Turbo GT and the two-door GT convertible.

The 2.3L four-cylinder was the base engine. The 3.3L inline was finally replaced by a new V-6, the 3.8L. This was an all-new design which featured aluminum cylinder heads. Porting was similar to that found on the 351C 2V heads, though the valves were not canted. Rated at 112 hp, it came only with the SelectShift automatic transmission.

The 2.3L Turbo surfaced again, this time as part of the Turbo GT, meaning that you could only get this engine if you ordered the three-door Turbo GT. It was not available with any other Mustang model. The 2.3L Turbo GT, rated at 145 hp, was superior to Ford's earlier turbocharging attempt. The engine featured Electronic Fuel Injection and its earlier reliability problems had been licked. However, it was overshadowed by the born-again 5.0L HO.

Development continued on the 5.0L HO. In 1983 guise, the two-barrel carburetor was trashed in favor of a Holley 600 cfm four-barrel mounted on an aluminum intake manifold—just like the old days! Horsepower jumped to 175.

To improve the GT's handling, the rear stabilizer bar was increased slightly in size, to .67 inch. However, the 1983's improvement in handling mostly can be attributed to larger sized tires. The standard GT tires went from a 185/75Rx14 to a 205/70HTx14 which were lower in profile and wider. Similarly, the TRX Michelins were increased to a P220/55R 390.

The GT's hood scoop changed ends again; this time the opening faced the rear.

The convertible, the first in ten years, came with a power top that had a glass backlite. Standard was the 3.8L V–6 and all the GLX features. Also available was the GT convertible. Convertibles were built by Cars & Concepts for Ford.

1983 was the last year that the 8-track player was offered, due to the waning popularity of the 8-track tape medium.

Two roof treatments were available—a flip-up open air sunroof and the T-tops. The Carriage Roof option, no longer necessary, was deleted from the option list.

*1983 convertible GT* Ford Motor Co.

# Chapter 20

# 1984 Mustang

## Production Figures

| | |
|---|---|
| 66B 2dr Sedan | 37,680 |
| 66B 2dr Convertible | 17,600 |
| 61B 3dr Hatchback | 86,200 |
| Total | 141,480 |

**1984 Mustang 20th Anniversary Edition**

| | |
|---|---|
| 3dr Turbo GT | 350 |
| 3dr 5.0L GT | 3,333 |
| 2dr Convertible Turbo GT | 104 |
| 2dr Convertible 5.0L GT | 1,213 |
| Ford VIP Convertibles | 15 |
| Ford of Canada (total) | 245 |
| Total | 5,260 |

Source: 20th Anniversary Registry

## Serial Numbers

1FABP26A6DF000001

1FA — Ford Motor Co.

B — Restraint system (B-active belts)

P — Passenger car

26 — Body code (26-2dr sedan, 27-2dr convertible, 28-3dr hatchback)

A — Engine code

6 — Check digit which varies

D — Year (D-1984)

F — Assembly plant (F-Dearborn)

000001 — Consecutive unit number

### Location

Stamped on riveted plate on driver's side of dash, visible through the windshield; certification label attached to rear face of driver's door.

### Engine Codes

A — 2.3L 1V 4 cyl 88 hp

T — 2.3L EFI 4 cyl 145 hp (Turbo GT)

W — 2.3L EFI 4 cyl 175 hp (SVO)

3 — 3.8L EFI V-6 120 hp

F — 5.0L EFI V-8 165 hp

M — 5.0L 4V V-8 175 hp (HO)

## 1984 Mustang Prices

| | Retail |
|---|---|
| 2dr L Sedan, P26 | $7,089.00 |
| 3dr L Sedan, P28 | 7,260.00 |
| 2dr LX Sedan, P26/602 | 7,281.00 |
| 3dr LX Sedan, P28/602 | 7,487.00 |
| 2dr LX Convertible, P27/602 | 11,840.00 |
| 3dr GT Sedan, P28/932 | 9,774.00 |
| 2dr GT Convertible, P27/932 | 13,247.00 |
| 3dr Turbo GT Sedan, P28/932 | 9,958.00 |

| | |
|---|---:|
| 2dr Turbo GT Convertible, P27/932 | 13,441.00 |
| 3dr SV0 P28/939/99T | 15,585.00 |
| 3.8L EFI 6 cyl engine (std. LX Convertible) | 409.00 |
| 5.0L 4V H0 8 cyl package/5–speed transmission (std. on GT except Turbo GT) | |
|    LX Convertible | 727.00 |
|    All other models | 1,574.00 |
| SelectShift automatic transmission (std. LX Convertible) | 439.00 |
| Automatic overdrive | 551.00 |
| Optional axle ratio | N/C |
| Traction-Lok axle | 95.00 |
| Tires, extra charge for four: | |
|    P185/75Rx14 WSW | 72.00 |
|    P195/75Rx14 WSW | 109.00 |
|    P205/70VRx14 BSW | 224.00 |
| Air conditioner, SelectAire | 743.00 |
| Battery, heavy-duty | 27.00 |
| Bodyside protection, lower | 41.00 |
| Bracket, front license plate | N/C |
| Brakes, power front disc | 93.00 |
| Competition Preparation option (SV0) | (1,253.00) |
| Console | 191.00 |
| Defroster, rear window electric | 140.00 |
| Floor mats, front carpet color-keyed | 22.00 |
| Glass, tinted complete | 110.00 |
| Heater, engine block immersion | 18.00 |
| Light Convenience Group | |
|    LX and GT | 55.00 |
|    All other models | 88.00 |
| Lock Group, power | 177.00 |
| Mirror, righthand remote-control | 46.00 |
| Moldings, rocker panel, black | 39.00 |
| Paint treatment, lower Tu-tone | 116.00 |
| Paint, special Tu-tone | |
|    L | 189.00 |
|    LX | 150.00 |
| Radio, AM/FM stereo | 109.00 |
| Radio, AM/FM stereo with cassette tape | 222.00 |
| AM radio, credit option | (39.00) |
| Sound system, premium | 151.00 |
| Roof, flip-up open air | 315.00 |
| Roof, "T" | 1,074.00 |
| Speed control, fingertip | 176.00 |
| Steering, power | 202.00 |
| Steering wheel, tilt | 110.00 |
| Suspension package, handling | 252.00 |
| Wheel covers, four wire style | 98.00 |
| Wheels, four cast aluminum | 354.00 |
| Wheels, four cast metric aluminum, P220/55R390 Michelin TRX BSW tires | |
|    L & LX | 551.00 |

| | |
|---|---|
| With 5.0L engine | 327.00 |
| GT | (27.00) |
| Wheels with trim rings, four styled steel | 78.00 |
| Windows, power side | |
| Convertible | 272.00 |
| All others | 198.00 |
| Windshield wipers, interval | 50.00 |
| Emission system, Calif. | 99.00 |
| Emission system, high altitude | N/C |
| Metallic glow paint | 54.00 |
| Cloth articulated sport seats | 366.00 |
| Vinyl seat trim | |
| L | 29.00 |
| LX & GT | 29.00 |
| Leather seat trim (Convertible only) | 415.00 |
| SVO | 189.00 |

## 1984 Exterior Colors

| Colors | Code |
|---|---|
| Black | 1C |
| Silver Metallic | 1E |
| Bright Canyon Red | 27 |
| Dark Academy Blue Metallic | 5C |
| Light Desert Tan | 8Q |
| Oxford White | 9L |
| Dark Charcoal Metallic | 9W |
| Medium Canyon Red Glow | 2B |
| Light Academy Blue Glow | 35 |
| Bright Copper Glow | 9C |
| Desert Tan Glow | 9J |

## 1984 Interior Trim

| Trim | Code |
|---|---|
| Charcoal | A |
| Cadet Blue | B |
| Canyon Red | D |
| Desert Tan | H |
| White/Red (Convertible) | N |
| White/Blue (Convertible) | Q |
| White/Charcoal (Convertible) | W |

## 1984 Mustang Facts

Model lineup changed for 1984. The base two-door and three-door Mustangs were L models. Upgraded two-door and three-door models, including the convertible, were LX Mustangs. GT Mustangs were available in three-door and convertible form, as were Turbo GT Mustangs. Midway through the model year, the 1984½ SVO Mustang was introduced. SVO stands for Special Vehicle Operations, a Ford unit formed in 1981 which was assigned the task of building a performance parts program and developing special high-performance street cars.

Exterior and interior styling was basically a carryover from 1983. Engine availability was the same, too, but there were some changes on the 3.8L V-6 and 5.0L HO. The 3.8L V-6 came with throttle body Electronic Fuel Injection and, again, this was the standard engine on the LX convertible. GT Mustangs with the automatic transmission got Ford's new four-speed automatic overdrive but the engine was equipped with a new intake system. Rather than using the 600 cfm Holley carburetor, it came with throttle body EFI, which brought its horsepower rating down to

165. Factory literature listed dual exhaust versions of the 5.0L as a mid-year introduction, but these were never made available.

The Turbo GT Mustangs were unchanged from 1983.

The standard transmission on the GTs was the Borg-Warner T-5, a five-speed manual overdrive, which gave the Mustang GT (and SVO) driver far more flexibility.

The big news was the 1984½ SVO Mustang, designed to deliver superior performance while appealing to a more sophisticated buyer. The heart of the SVO was yet another version of the 2.3L four-cylinder. Similar to the Turbo GT engine, this engine came with an intercooler and EFI to boost hp to 175. Maximum boost was 14 psi, which was electronically controlled. Other features included a revised front suspension with Koni adjustable shocks, four wheel disc brakes, the Quadra-Shock rear suspension (from the Thunderbird Turbo Coupe) and 16x7 inch aluminum wheels with P225/50VR Goodyear NCT tires. The SVO was equipped with articulated front seats with adjustable lumbar support, leather-wrapped steering wheel and a premium stereo system. Major options were air conditioning, power windows and locks, cassette, pop-up sunroof and leather interior. Exterior colors were black, charcoal, silver and red, all with a charcoal interior. Externally, the SVO got a unique grille, functional hood scoop, wheel spats in front of the rear wheelwell openings and a large biplane rear spoiler. It was a nice package, but its high price—some $6,000 more than the Mustang GT—limited its appeal.

The other special of 1984 was the 20th Anniversary Edition Mustang which commemorated the Mustang's 20th anniversary. They were all Mustang GTs, three-doors and convertibles powered by the 302 HO or Turbo GT. Paint color was Oxford White with Canyon Red interiors. The 20th also came with articulated front seats but without the adjustable lumbar support. The rest of the package consisted of a rocker panel tape treatment with GT350 lettering, original (1965) type front fender emblems and two 20th Anniversary dash panel badges. The first of these, a horseshoe medallion, was located on the passenger's side of the dash. About three to four months after purchase, the owner was sent a form to fill out so that the second medallion could be obtained. This one read "Limited Edition" followed by a serial number (unrelated to the car's VIN) and, below that, the owner's name. A total of 5,260 Anniversary Editions were built.

The standard GT tires were upgraded to a V rating, good for 130 mph and above. The TRX wheels/tires were still optional, but it was their last year. From 1985 on, Goodyear Eagles were used on the GT.

The adjustable articulated seats were optional on all Mustangs.

Ford took over production of the convertible Mustangs from Cars & Concepts, making 1984 and later convertibles true factory convertibles.

From 1984 on, Mustangs were equipped with Ford's EEC-IV (electronic engine control system), monitoring all engine functions. The EEC-IV was designed to meet emissions regulations while maximizing performance.

*1984 20th Anniversary convertible*

*1984 20th Anniversary three-door* Stephen Jacobs

*1984½ SVO* Ford Motor Co.

# Chapter 21

# 1985 Mustang

## Production Figures

| | | | |
|---|---|---|---|
| 66B 2dr Sedan | 56,781 | 61B 3dr Hatchback | 84,623 |
| 66B 2dr Convertible | 15,110 | Total | 156,514 |

## Serial Numbers

1FABP26A6FF000001

1FA — Ford Motor Co.

B — Restraint system (B-active belts)

P — Passenger car

26 — Body code (26-2dr sedan, 27-2dr convertible, 28-3dr hatchback)

A — Engine code

6 — Check digit which varies

F — Year (F-1985)

F — Assembly plant (F-Dearborn)

000001 — Consecutive unit number

### Location

Stamped on riveted plate on driver's side of dash, visible through the windshield; certification label attached on rear face of driver's door.

### Engine Codes

A — 2.3L 1V 4 cyl 88 hp

W — 2.3L EFI 4 cyl 205 hp (SVO)

3 — 3.8L EFI V-6 120 hp

M — 5.0L EFI/4V V-8 165/210 hp (HO)

## 1985 Mustang Prices — Retail

| | Retail |
|---|---|
| 2dr LX Sedan, P26/602 | $6,989.00 |
| 3dr LX Sedan, P28/602 | 7,509.00 |
| 2dr LX Convertible, P27/602 | 12,237.00 |
| 3dr GT Sedan, P28/932 | 10,224.00 |
| 2dr GT Convertible, P27/932 | 13,930.00 |
| 3dr SVO, P28/937 | 14,806.00 |
| 3.8L EFI 6 cyl engine (std. LX Convertible) | 454.00 |
| 5.0L 4V HO 8 cyl package (std. on GT) | |
| LX Convertible | 172.00 |
| LX Sedans | 1,020.00 |
| 5-speed manual overdrive (std. GT & SVO) | 124.00 |
| SelectShift automatic transmission (std. LX Convertible) | 470.00 |
| Automatic overdrive | |
| LX | 706.00 |
| GT | 582.00 |
| Optional axle ratio | N/C |

| | |
|---|---|
| Traction-Lok axle | 100.00 |
| Tires, extra charge for four: | |
|    P205/70Rx14 WSW | 109.00 |
|    P205/70VRx14 BSW performance | 238.00 |
|    P225/60VRx15 BSW cast aluminum wheels | 665.00 |
| Air conditioner, manual | 762.00 |
| Battery, heavy-duty | 27.00 |
| Bracket, front license plate | N/C |
| Competition Preparation option (SVO) | (1,451.00) |
| Console | 191.00 |
| Defroster, rear window electric | 145.00 |
| Glass, tinted complete | 115.00 |
| Heater, engine block immersion | 18.00 |
| Light Group | 55.00 |
| Lock Group, power | |
|    LX | 215.00 |
|    GT | 182.00 |
| Paint treatment, lower Tu-tone | 116.00 |
| Radio, electronic AM/FM stereo with cassette tape | 300.00 |
| Radio, credit option | (148.00) |
| Sound system, premium | 138.00 |
| Roof, flip-up open air | 315.00 |
| Roof, "T" | 1,100.00 |
| Speed control, fingertip | 176.00 |
| Spoiler, single wing | N/C |
| Steering wheel, tilt | 115.00 |
| Wheel covers, four wire style | 98.00 |
| Wheels, four styled road | 178.00 |
| Windows, power side | |
|    Convertible | 282.00 |
|    All others | 207.00 |
| Emissions system, Calif. | 99.00 |
| Emission system, high altitude | N/C |
| Leather articulated sport seats | |
|    LX Convertible | 780.00 |
|    GT Convertible | 415.00 |
| Vinyl seat trim | 29.00 |
| Leather seat trim, SVO | 189.00 |

| **1985 Exterior Colors** | **Code** | **1985 Interior Trim** | **Code** |
|---|---|---|---|
| Black | 1C | Charcoal | A |
| Medium Charcoal | 1B | Regatta Blue | B |
| Canyon Red | 2C | Canyon Red | D |
| Pastel Regatta Blue | 3M | Sand Beige | Y |
| Oxford Grey | 1U | White/Red | |
| Sand Beige | 8L |   (Convertible) | N |
| Silver | 1Q | White/Blue | |
| Jalapena Red | 2R |   (Convertible) | Q |
| Oxford White | 9L | White/Charcoal | |
| Dark Sable | 8Y |   (Convertible) | W |
| Medium Regatta Blue | 3Y | | |

## 1985 Mustang Facts

Emulating the SVO's look, all 1985 Mustangs got a new frontal treatment along with different bodyside moldings. Interior configuration was still the same. The Turbo GT was dropped, but the SVO was still available. The SVO was updated during the model year and rereleased as a 1985½ model.

Besides the SVO, Mustang models were limited to two-door, three-door and convertible in LX trim with the GT available as a three-door or convertible. Of course, the LX could be optioned out with the 5.0L HO and the GT's 15x7 wheels/tires to GT specs but at a higher cost.

Engine choice was limited to the standard 2.3L, the optional 3.8L V-6 (standard on the LX convertible) and the powerhouse 5.0L HO.

The biggest and most significant changes occurred on the Mustang GT as the muscle-car wars, 1980's style, were heating up.

The engine compartment of the GT looked outwardly the same. Upon a closer look the new exhaust headers were evident. These were stainless steel headers and not the typical so-called free-flowing cast iron exhaust manifolds. Coupled to a true dual exhaust system, with dual catalytic converters, horsepower jumped to 210. Internally, the 5.0L got a hotter camshaft with roller lifters. Contributing to the 210 hp total was a new accessory drive system which slowed down the air conditioner, alternator and power steering pump to half speed above idle.

The T-5 transmission got shorter gear throws for quicker response but what really improved the GT's road manners was the addition of the Quadra-Shock rear, a larger rear stabilizer bar and the new Goodyear tires. These were the Goodyear Eagle P225/60VR-15 unidirectional Gatorbacks mounted on new 15x7 inch aluminum wheels. These big tires, wider than any previous Mustang tires, helped the Mustang handle better.

In the interior, the articulated seats were standard as was the SVO's steering wheel. The exterior GT graphics were slightly subdued, using a dark charcoal treatment rather than the previous blacked-out treatment.

The GT was also available with an automatic overdrive transmission; however it did not use the same engine. This was the EFI version of the 5.0L rated at 165 hp. This engine used throttle body injection which is not to be confused with the multi-port injection available from 1986 on.

The SVO was updated as a mid-year model. Visually, the SVO got flush headlamps, but the important changes were not visual. The engine, through the use of a higher performance camshaft, reworked intake manifold and Turbocharger, a freer flowing exhaust system, larger fuel injection nozzles and a one-pound increase in Turbo boost, was rated at an impressive 205 hp. Through the use of redesigned brackets, the engine was far smoother, too. The suspension was tighter with 14.7:1 ratio steering, stiffer shocks and teflon-lined stabilizer bar bushings which contributed to improved handling, as did the Goodyear Eagle tires replacing the NCTs.

The rear wing spoiler (GT-type) was a no-cost option on the LX three-door hatchbacks.

The T-roofs were still available as was the flip-up open air sunroof.

Ninety Twister IIs were sold through the Kansas City sales district. Strictly a cosmetic package, it consisted of exterior graphics and a special dash plaque. Seventy-six were three-door GTs while fourteen were GT convertibles. Colors were limited to Bright Red, Medium Canyon Red, Oxford White and Silver Metallic.

*1985–86 three-door*

# Chapter 22

# 1986 Mustang

## Production Figures

| | | | |
|---|---|---|---|
| 66B 2dr Sedan | 83,774 | 61B 3dr Hatchback | 117,690 |
| 66B 2dr Convertible | 22,946 | Total | 224,410 |

## Serial Numbers

1FABP26A6GF000001

1FA — Ford Motor Co.

B — Restraint system (B-active belts)

P — Passenger car

26 — Body code (26-2dr sedan, 27-2dr convertible, 28-3dr hatchback)

A — Engine code

6 — Check digit which varies

G — Year (G-1986)

F — Plant (F-Dearborn)

000001 — Consecutive unit number

### Location

Stamped on riveted plate on driver's side of dash, visible through the windshield; certification label attached on rear face of driver's door.

### Engine Codes

S — 2.3L 1V 4 cyl 88 hp

W — 2.3L EFI 4 cyl 205 hp (SVO)

3 — 3.8L EFI V-6 120 hp

M — 5.0L EFI V-8 200 hp (HO)

## 1986 Mustang Prices — Retail

| | Retail |
|---|---|
| 2dr LX Sedan, P26 | $7,420.00 |
| 2dr LX Hatchback, P28 | 7,974.00 |
| 2dr LX Convertible, P27 | 13,214.00 |
| 2dr GT Hatchback, P28 | 11,102.00 |
| 2dr GT Convertible, P27 | 14,945.00 |
| 2dr SVO, P28 | 15,272.00 |
| 3.8L EFI 6 cyl (std. LX Convertible) | 565.00 |
| 5.0L EFI HO 8 cyl package (std. GT) | |
|     LX Convertible | 646.00 |
|     LX Sedan or Convertible | 1,211.00 |
| 5-speed manual overdrive (std. GT) | |
|     LX Sedan or Hatchback | 124.00 |
|     LX Convertible | (410.00) |
| SelectShift automatic (std. LX Convertible) | 534.00 |

| | |
|---|---|
| Automatic overdrive | |
|    LX Sedan or Hatchback | 771.00 |
|    LX Convertible | 237.00 |
|    GT | 646.00 |
| Tires, extra charge for four: | |
|    P205/70Rx14 WSW | 118.00 |
|    P225/60VRx15 BSW cast aluminum wheels | 674.00 |
| Air conditioner, manual | 788.00 |
| Battery, heavy-duty | 27.00 |
| Bracket, front license plate | N/C |
| Console | 191.00 |
| Competition Preparation option (SVO) | 1,451.00 |
| Defroster, rear window | 145.00 |
| Glass, tinted complete | 120.00 |
| Heater, engine block immersion | 18.00 |
| Hood graphic credit | N/C |
| Light Group | 55.00 |
| Lock Group, power | |
|    LX | 244.00 |
|    GT | 206.00 |
| Paint, lower charcoal accent | 116.00 |
| Radio, AM/FM stereo with cassette tape | 157.00 |
| Radio, electronic AM/FM stereo with cassette tape | 310.00 |
| Radio, credit option | (157.00) |
| Sound system, premium | 138.00 |
| Roof, flip-up open air | 355.00 |
| Roof, "T" | 1,120.00 |
| Speed control | 176.00 |
| Spoiler, single rear wing | N/C |
| Steering wheel, tilt | 124.00 |
| Wheel covers, four wire style | 98.00 |
| Wheels, four styled road | 178.00 |
| Windows, power side | |
|    Convertibles | 296.00 |
|    All others | 222.00 |
| Emission system, Calif. | 99.00 |
| Emission system, high altitude | N/C |
| Leather articulated sport seats | |
|    LX Convertible | 780.00 |
|    GT Convertible | 415.00 |
| Vinyl seat trim | 29.00 |

| 1986 Exterior Colors | Code | 1986 Exterior Colors | Code |
|---|---|---|---|
| Black | 1C | Dark Sage | 4E |
| Dark Grey Metallic | 1B | Dark Slate Metallic | 4M |
| Silver Metallic | 1E | Shadow Blue Metallic | 7B |
| Medium Canyon Red Metallic | 2C | Sand Beige | 8A |
| | | Dark Clove Metallic | 8Y |
| Bright Red | 2A | Oxford White | 9L |
| Light Regatta Blue Metallic | 3J | | |

| 1986 Interior Trim | Code | 1986 Interior Trim | Code |
|---|---|---|---|
| Charcoal | A | White/Blue (Convertible) | Q |
| Regatta Blue | B | | |
| Canyon Red | D | White/Charcoal (Convertible) | W |
| Sand Beige | Y | | |
| White/Red (Convertible) | N | | |

## 1986 Mustang Facts

1986 was the last year for the SVO. For the typical Mustang buyer, the 302 HO powered GT provided similar performance for a lot less money.

Model line-up was simplified—LX Mustangs could be had in a two-door, three-door and convertible, and the GT in either the three-door hatchback or convertible. This simplification process would be continued in the following years with the number of options available decreasing each year.

Besides minor trim and color changes, Mustang styling was unchanged from 1985.

The 5.0L HO got a new intake setup—sequential multi-port electronic fuel injection—but a lower horsepower rating than 1985, 200 hp versus 210 hp. Other engine changes included redesigned cylinder heads, beefed up block and a more efficient water pump.

The GT's hood graphics could now be deleted—a no-charge option. The rear wing spoiler for the hatchbacks was still a no-cost option.

The 7.5 inch rear was replaced by the stronger 8.8 in. integral carrier unit from Ford's full size cars on the GT. Standard ratio was 2.73:1 with 3.08:1 optional. The 3.27:1 ratio was optional only with the automatic overdrive transmission.

# Chapter 23

# 1987 Mustang

## Production Figures

| | | | |
|---|---|---|---|
| 66B 2dr Sedan | 43,257 | 61B 3dr Hatchback | 94,441 |
| 66B 2dr Convertible | 32,074 | Total | 159,145 |

## Serial Numbers

1FABP40A6HF000001

1FA — Ford Motor Co.

B — Restraint system (B-active belts)

P — Passenger car

40 — Body code (40-2dr LX, 41-3dr LX, 42-3dr GT, 44-2dr LX convertible, 45-2dr GT convertible)

A — Engine code

6 — Check digit which varies

H — Year (H-1987)

F — Plant (F-Dearborn)

000001 — Consecutive unit number

### Location

Stamped on riveted plate on driver's side of dash, visible through the windshield; certification label attached to left B-pillar.

### Engine Codes

S — 2.3L 1V 4 cyl 88 hp

M — 5.0L EFI V-8 225 hp (HO)

| 1987 Mustang Prices | Retail |
|---|---|
| 2 dr LX Sedan, P40 | $8,271.00 |
| 2 dr LX Hatchback, P41 | 8,690.00 |
| 2 dr LX Convertible, P44 | 13,052.00 |
| 2 dr GT Hatchback, P42 | 12,106.00 |
| 2 dr GT Convertible, P45 | 15,852.00 |
| 5.0L EFI HO 8 cyl package (std. GT) | 1,885.00 |
| Automatic overdrive | |
|     LX | 515.00 |
|     GT | 515.00 |
| Tires, extra charge for four P195/75Rx14 WSW | 82.00 |
| Air conditioner, manual | 788.00 |
| Battery, heavy-duty | 27.00 |
| Bracket, front license plate | N/C |
| Defroster, rear window | 145.00 |
| Heater, engine block immersion | 18.00 |
| Lock Group, power | |
|     LX | 244.00 |
|     GT | 206.00 |
| Mirrors, dual electric remote | 60.00 |

| | |
|---|---:|
| Mirrors, dual illuminated visor | 100.00 |
| Molding, bodyside insert stripe | 49.00 |
| Radio, electronic AM/FM with cassette tape | 137.00 |
| Sound system, premium | 168.00 |
| Radio credit option | (206.00) |
| Graphic equalizer | 218.00 |
| Roof, flip-up open air | 355.00 |
| Roof, "T", LX | 1,798.00 |
| GT | 1,618.00 |
| Speed control | 176.00 |
| Steering wheel, tilt | 124.00 |
| Wheel covers, four wire style | 98.00 |
| Wheels, four styled road | 178.00 |
| Windows, power side | |
| Sedan & Hatchback | 222.00 |
| Convertibles | 296.00 |
| Emission system, Calif. | 99.00 |
| Emission system, high altitude | N/C |
| Leather articulated sport seats | |
| LX Convertible | 780.00 |
| GT Convertible | 415.00 |
| Vinyl seat trim | 29.00 |
| Lower titanium accent treatment (GT only) | N/C |

| 1987 Exterior Colors | Code | 1987 Interior Trim | Code |
|---|---|---|---|
| Black | 1C | Regatta Blue | B |
| Dark Grey Metallic | 9R | Scarlet | D |
| Light Grey | 1K | Smoke | G |
| Scarlet Red | 2D | Sand Beige | Y |
| Medium Cabernet | 2H | White/Scarlet | |
| Medium Shadow Blue | | (Convertible) | N |
| Metallic | 3R | White/Blue | |
| Medium Yellow | 66 | (Convertible) | Q |
| Dark Shadow Blue | | White/Smoke | |
| Metallic | 7N | (Convertible) | U |
| Bright Regatta Blue | | | |
| Metallic | 7H | | |
| Sand Beige | 8L | | |
| Dark Clove Metallic | 5H | | |
| Oxford White | 9L | | |

# 1987 Mustang Facts

Entering the tenth year with the same basic platform, Ford gave the Mustang a much needed facelift, emulating the aero-look of the company's other offerings. From the rear or from the side, the Mustang still looked like the same old Mustang, but at least from the front, it looked different.

The new GT achieved a totally different look through a redesigned nose with the flush fitting headlights. A ground effect skirt package with scoops on front of each wheel opening, extended around to the rear giving the car a much lower appearance. On the hatch sat a large rear wing, but the most noticeable change was the unusual louvered rear taillights.

The redesigned dash gave the Mustang a more modern look. Instrumentation was complete: fuel, water temperature, oil pressure, voltmeter, tachometer and a speedometer which still read only to 85 mph. The GTs got the articulated seats with power lumbar support and adjustable under-thigh support. Air conditioning controls, also new, were relocated in the center console top above the radio.

The standard engine on all LX Mustangs was still the 2.3L. The only optional engine (as the 3.8L V-6 was dropped) was the 5.0L HO. Thanks to a larger throttle body and better flowing cylinder heads derived from the 5.0 used on Ford trucks, the HO pumped out a very strong 225 hp (220 with the AOD) with 300 pounds-feet of torque.

The five-speed manual transmission was standard equipment across the board. With the 5.0L, axle ratios were unchanged from before, 2.73:1 with the five-speed or 3.08:1 with the optional automatic overdrive.

The suspension was also improved with many parts once used on the SVO. Increased wheel travel coupled with alignment changes gave the Mustang a better feel. Steering ratios, 20:1 for the LX and 14.7:1 on the GT and 5.0L-equipped LXs, was unchanged from 1986. Rear stabilizer bar size was upgraded to .82 inch on the 5.0L.

Front disc brakes were increased to 10.9 inches diameter for better braking, though the rear brakes were still 9-inch drums.

The GTs came with a new aluminum turbine wheel. The ten-hole aluminum wheels used on the 1986 GTs now became the standard wheel on Mustangs equipped with the 5.0L HO engine package.

The tilt-wheel was standard on the GTs. A new option for 1987 was the graphic equalizer. The only optional radio was the electronic AM/FM cassette stereo unit.

A lower titanium paint accent treatment was a no-cost option on the GT.

Leather was optional only on the LX and GT convertibles.

*1987 LX convertible* Ford Motor Co.

*1987 GT*

# Chapter 24

# 1988 Mustang

## Production Figures

| | | | |
|---|---|---|---|
| 66B 2dr Sedan | 53,221 | 61B 3dr Hatchback | 125,930 |
| 66B 2dr Convertible | 32,074 | Total | 211,225 |

## Serial Numbers

1FABP40A6JF000001

1FA — Ford Motor Co.

B — Restraint system (B-active belts)

P — Passenger car

40 — Body code (40-2dr LX, 41-3dr LX, 42-3dr GT, 44-2dr LX convertible, 45-2dr GT convertible)

A — Engine code

6 — Check digit which varies

J — Year (J-1988)

F — Plant (F-Dearborn)

000001 — Consecutive unit number

### Location

Stamped on riveted plate on driver's side of dash, visible through the windshield; certification label attached to rear face of driver's door.

### Engine Codes

S — 2.3L 1V 4 cyl 88 hp

M — 5.0L EFI V-8 225 hp(HO)

## 1988 Mustang Prices

| | Retail |
|---|---|
| 2dr LX Sedan, P40 | $8,835.00 |
| 2dr LX Hatchback, P41 | 9,341.00 |
| 2dr LX Convertible, P44 | 13,702.00 |
| 2dr GT Hatchback, P42 | 12,745.00 |
| 2dr GT Convertible, P45 | 16,610.00 |
| 5.0L EFI HO 8 cyl (std. GT) | 2,007.00 |
| Automatic overdrive | |
|    LX | 515.00 |
|    GT | 515.00 |
| Tires, extra charge for four P195/75Rx14 WSW | 82.00 |
| Air conditioner, manual | 788.00 |
| Bracket, front license plate | N/C |
| Defroster, rear window | 145.00 |
| Heater, engine block immersion | 18.00 |
| Lock Group, power | 237.00 |
| Mirrors, dual electric remote | 60.00 |
| Mirrors, dual illuminated visor | 100.00 |
| Molding, bodyside insert stripe | 49.00 |

| | |
|---|---|
| Radio, electronic AM/FM with cassette tape | 137.00 |
| Sound system, premium | 168.00 |
| Radio credit option | (206.00) |
| Graphic equalizer | 218.00 |
| Roof, flip-up open air | 355.00 |
| Speed control | 182.00 |
| Steering wheel, tilt | 124.00 |
| Wheel covers, four wire style | 178.00 |
| Wheels, four styled road | 178.00 |
| Windows, power side | 222.00 |
| Emission system, Calif. | 99.00 |
| Emission system, high altitude | N/C |
| Leather articulated sport seats | |
|    LX Convertible | 780.00 |
|    GT Convertible | 415.00 |
| Vinyl seat trim | 37.00 |
| Lower titanium accent treatment (GT only) | N/C |

## 1988 Exterior Colors

| Colors | Code |
|---|---|
| Black | 1C |
| Dark Grey | |
|    Metallic | 1D |
| Light Grey | 1K |
| Bright Red | 2I |
| Cabernet Red | 2H |
| Medium Shadow | |
|    Blue Metallic | 3R |
| Tropical Yellow | 66 |
| Deep Shadow Blue | |
|    Metallic | 7N |
| Bright Regatta Blue | |
|    Metallic | 7H |
| Almond | 6V |
| Oxford White | 9L |

## 1988 Interior Trim

| Trim | Code |
|---|---|
| Regatta Blue | B |
| Scarlet | D |
| Smoke | G |
| Sand Beige | Y |
| White/Scarlet | |
|    (Convertible) | N |
| White/Blue | |
|    (Convertible) | Q |
| White/Smoke | |
|    (Convertible) | U |

## 1988 Mustang Facts

No significant changes were made on the 1988 Mustang.

Although the T-roof was discontinued after the 1987 model year, a few early 1988s were built with it.

# Chapter 25

# 1989 Mustang

## Production Figures

| | | | |
|---|---|---|---|
| 66B 2dr Sedan | 50,560 | 61B 3dr Hatchback | 116,965 |
| 66B 2dr Convertible | 42,244 | Total | 209,769 |

## Serial Numbers

1FABP40A6KF000001

1FA — Ford Motor Co.

B — Restraint system (B-active belts)

P — Passenger car

40 — Body code (40-2dr LX, 41-3dr LX, 42-3dr GT, 44-2dr LX convertible, 45-2dr GT convertible)

A — Engine code

6 — Check digit which varies

K — Year (K-1989)

F — Assembly plant (F-Dearborn)

000001 — Consecutive unit number

### Location

Stamped on riveted plate on driver's side of dash, visible through the windshield; certification label attached on rear face of driver's door.

### Engine Codes

S — 2.3L 1V 4 cyl 88 hp

M — 5.0L EFI V-8 225 hp (HO)

## 1989 Mustang Prices

| | Retail |
|---|---|
| 2dr LX Sedan, P40 | $9,050.00 |
| 2dr LX Hatchback, P41 | 9,556.00 |
| 2dr LX Convertible, P44 | 14,140.00 |
| 2dr LX 5.0L Sport Sedan, P40 | 11,410.00 |
| 2dr LX 5.0L Sport Hatchback, P41 | 12,265.00 |
| 2dr LX 5.0L Sport Convertible, P44 | 17,001.00 |
| 2dr GT Hatchback, P42 | 13,272.00 |
| 2dr GT Convertible, P45 | 17,512.00 |
| Automatic overdrive | |
|    LX | 515.00 |
|    GT | 515.00 |
| Tires, extra charge for four P195/75Rx14 WSW | 82.00 |
| Air conditioner, manual | 807.00 |
| Bracket, front license plate | N/C |
| Defroster, rear window | 150.00 |
| Heater, engine block immersion | 20.00 |
| Lock Group, power | 246.00 |

| | |
|---|---|
| Mirrors, dual electric remote | 70.00 |
| Mirrors, dual illuminated visor | 100.00 |
| Molding, bodyside insert stripe | 61.00 |
| Radio, electronic AM/FM with cassette tape & clock | 137.00 |
| Sound system, premium | 168.00 |
| Radio credit option | (245.00-382.00)* |
| Roof, flip-up open air | 355.00 |
| Speed control | 191.00 |
| Steering wheel, tilt | 124.00 |
| Wheel covers, four wire style | 193.00 |
| Wheels, four styled road | 193.00 |
| Windows, power side | 232.00 |
| Emission system, Calif. | 100.00 |
| Emission system, high altitude | N/C |
| Leather articulated sport seats | |
|     LX Convertible | 855.00 |
|     LX 5.0L Sport Convertible or GT Convertible | 489.00 |
| Vinyl seat trim | 37.00 |
| Lower titanium accent treatment (GT only) | N/C |

    *Depending on equipment package

| 1989 Exterior Colors | Code | 1989 Interior Trim | Code |
|---|---|---|---|
| Black | 1C | Regatta Blue | B |
| Dark Grey Metallic | 1D | Scarlet | D |
| Light Grey | 1K | Smoke | G |
| Bright Red | 21 | Sand Beige | Y |
| Cabernet Red | 2H | White/Scarlet | |
| Medium Shadow Blue | |   (Convertible) | N |
|   Metallic | 3R | White/Blue | |
| Tropical Yellow | 66 |   (Convertible) | Q |
| Almond | 6V | White/Smoke | |
| Bright Regatta Blue | |   (Convertible) | U |
|   Metallic | 7H | | |
| Deep Shadow Blue | | | |
|   Metallic | 7N | | |
| Oxford White | 9L | | |

## 1989 Mustang Facts

    No significant changes were made on the 1989 Mustang.

    The graphic equalizer was not available in 1989.

    A clock function was added to the optional electronic AM/FM cassette stereo.

    The LX models with the optional 5.0L were renamed LX 5.0L Sport. During the model year, a 140 mph speedometer took the place of the standard 85 mph unit on 5.0L powered Mustangs.

# Chapter 26

# 1990 Mustang

## Serial Numbers
1FACP40A6LF000001
1FA — Ford Motor Co.
C — Restraint system (C-air bags & active belts)
P — Passenger car
40 — Body code (40-2dr LX, 41-3dr LX, 42-3dr GT, 44-2dr convertible, 45-GT convertible)
A — Engine code
6 — Check digit which varies
L — Year (L-1990)
F — Assembly plant (F-Dearborn)
000001 — Consecutive unit number

### Location
Stamped on riveted plate on driver's side of dash, visible through the windshield; certification label attached on rear face of driver's door.

### Engine Codes
S — 2.3L EFI 4 cyl 88 hp
M — 5.0L EFI V-8 225 hp(HO)

| 1990 Mustang Prices | Retail |
| --- | --- |
| 2dr LX Sedan, P40 | $9,753.00 |
| 2dr LX Hatchback, P41 | 10,259.00 |
| 2dr LX Convertible, P44 | 14,810.00 |
| 2dr LX 5.0L Sport Sedan, P40 | 12,222.00 |
| 2dr LX 5.0L Sport Hatchback, P41 | 13,065.00 |
| 2dr LX 5.0L Sport Convertible, P44 | 17,796.00 |
| 2dr GT Hatchback, P42 | 14,044.00 |
| 2dr GT Convertible, P45 | 18,418.00 |
| Automatic overdrive | 539.00 |
| Tires, extra charge for four P195/75Rx24 WSW on LX | 82.00 |
| Air conditioner, manual control | 807.00 |
| Defroster, rear window | 150.00 |
| Heater, engine block immersion | 20.00 |
| Mirrors, dual illuminated visor | 100.00 |
| Power equipment group (std. on convertibles) | 507.00 |
| Roof, flip-up open air | 355.00 |
| Radio, electronic AM/FM with cassette & clock | 137.00 |
| Sound system, premium | 168.00 |
| Radio credit option* | (245.00–550.00) |
| Speed control | 191.00 |
| Wheel covers, wire style | 193.00 |
| Emissions system, Calif. | 100.00 |

| | |
|---|---|
| Paint, clearcoat | 91.00 |
| Lower titanium accent treatment (GT only) | 159.00 |
| Leather seating surface, articulated sport seats | 489.00 |
| Vinyl seat trim | 37.00 |

*Depending on option package

## 1990 Exterior Colors

| Colors | Code |
|---|---|
| Cabernet Red | EH |
| Bright Red | EP |
| Black | YC |
| Oxford White | YO |
| Bright Yellow | AG |
| Wild Strawberry | EL |
| Crystal Blue | MA |
| Twilight Blue | MK |
| Deep Emerald Green | YF* |
| Deep Titanium | YU |
| Light Titanium | YF |

*On LX 5.0L Convertible Special only

## 1990 Interior Trim

| Trim | Code |
|---|---|
| Titanium | A |
| Crystal Blue | B |
| Scarlet | D |
| Ebony | J |
| White/Titanium | L |
| White/Scarlet | N |
| White/Crystal Blue | W |
| White | |

## Convertible Top Colors

Black
Dark Blue
White

## 1990 Mustang Facts

Again, no significant styling or mechanical changes were made on the 1990 Mustangs, save for the driver's side air bag.

Interior changes included the deletion of the center console armrest, the addition of door trim map pockets and a driver's footrest on the LX.

The standard wheel covers are a finned design, with the wire wheel covers optional on the LX.

The LX 5.0L and GT Mustangs got 140 mph speedometers.

A limited edition convertible, 2,000 units, for 1990½ is planned. It will come in deep emerald green clearcoat metallic exterior paint and a white interior.

*1990 three-door LX 5.0 Sport* Ford Motor Co.

# Chapter 27

# 1965 Shelby Mustang

## Production Figures

| | | | |
|---|---|---|---|
| Street prototype | 1 | Competition models | 35 |
| Street production models | 515 | Drag cars | 9 |
| Competition prototypes | 2 | Total | 562 |

### Shelby VIN

SFM5S001

SFM — Shelby Ford Mustang

5 — Year (1965)

S — Street, R — Race

001 — Consecutive unit number,
001 to 562

#### Location

On pop-riveted plate on driver's side inner fender panel over Ford VIN; also stamped on passenger's side inner fender panel halfway between firewall and radiator.

### Ford VIN

5R09K000001

5 — Last digit of model year

R — Assembly plant
(R-San Jose)

09 — Body code (09-2dr fastback)

K — Engine code
(271 hp 289 ci V-8)

000001 — Consecutive unit number

#### Location

Underneath Shelby VIN plate; on driver's and passenger's side inner fender panels at outside edge near shock tower; can only be viewed if fenders are removed; on original engine block, beneath front exhaust port on passenger side.

### Carburetor

Holley R-3259

### Distributor

C5GF-12127-A, C50F-12127-E, C5AZ-12127-EEZ

### 1965 Shelby Prices                     Retail

| | |
|---|---|
| Street | $4,547.00 |
| Race | 5,995.00 |

### 1965 Shelby Colors

All 1965 Shelby Mustangs were painted Wimbledon White, code M. Interior was black.

### 1965 Shelby GT350 Facts

1965 Shelby Mustangs can be identified by their blue rocker panel GT350 stripes. The wide blue racing stripes running the length of the car were mostly dealer installed but some were installed at the factory. With the exception of the stock Mustang gas cap and relocated grille emblem (the far left of the grille), all other Mustang emblems were removed. Some GT350s did have a GT350 emblem on the left side of the taillight panel. The Shelby's hood was different from stock as it was made from fiberglass and has a functional hood scoop. Some hoods came with steel frames and fiberglass skins.

Most noticeable in the interior was the pod attached to the dash top which housed a tachometer and oil pressure gauge. All 1965s did not have a rear seat; a fiberglass shelf took its place and was also the location for the spare tire. Large, 3 inch competition seatbelts replaced the stock belts. Three types of wooden steering wheels were used. Early cars came with 16 inch diameter wheels with slotted spokes; later cars came with 15 inch wheels with either slotted spokes or three holes in each spoke.

The engine was the stock High Performance 271 hp 289 with Shelby modifications which boosted horsepower to 306. These were an aluminum high-rise intake manifold with a 715 cfm Holley four-barrel carburetor and steel Tri-Y headers exiting to a dual exhaust system using glasspack mufflers and exiting in front of the rear wheels. The exception here was cars built after July 6, 1965 for delivery to California, Florida or New Jersey which got a rear-exiting exhaust system. Cobra valve covers and a larger capacity aluminum Cobra oil pan rounded out the package.

Transmission was an aluminum case Borg Warner T-10. The 9 inch rear had 3.89 gears (but others were available) and they all had a Detroit Locker differential. A drive shaft safety loop was standard equipment. Additional rear axle control was achieved through the use of traction bars and travel-limiting cables.

Shock absorbers were the renowned Koni adjustable units. The use of a Monte Carlo bar, attached between the shock towers and a one-piece export brace, noticeably stiffened the GT350's front frame structure. All cars came with a lowered front suspension (1 inch) and, for better weight distribution, the battery was relocated to the trunk, at least for most cars between numbers 001 and 324.

Manual brakes and manual quick ratio steering were standard. Stock wheels were silver painted steel rims with chrome lug nuts with Goodyear 7.75x15 Blue Dot tires. Optional were the Cragar mags.

The "R" (race) version, in addition to all the street version features, got a fiberglass front lower apron, engine oil cooler, larger capacity radiator, front and rear brake cooling assemblies, 34 gallon gas tank, 3½ inch quick fill gas cap, electric fuel pump, large diameter exhaust pipes with no mufflers, five magnesium 15x7 wheels, revised wheel openings, Interior Safety Group (roll bar, shoulder harness, fire extinguisher, flame resistant interior, plastic rear window, aluminum framed sliding plastic side windows) complete instrumentation (tachometer, speedometer, oil pressure and temperature, water temperature and fuel pressure), and final track test and adjustments. The engine was further modified to produce 350 hp.

Cars with serial numbers 004-034 have no "S" designation on the VIN plate. All others are either "S" or "R."

*1965 Shelby GT350*

*Chapter 28*

# 1966 Shelby Mustang

## Production Figures

| | |
|---|---|
| GT350 | 1,370 |
| GT350H Hertz | 1,000 |
| GT350 Drag cars | 4 |
| GT350 Convertibles | 6* |
| Total | 2,380 |

*Does not include the 12 continuation convertibles built during 1980 through 1982

## Shelby VIN

SFM6S0001
SFM — Shelby Ford Mustang
6 — Last digit of model year
S — Street car
0001 — Consecutive unit number, 0001 to 2380

### Location

On plate pop-riveted on driver's side inner fender panel covering Ford VIN; also on passenger's side inner front fender panel halfway between radiator and firewall.

## Ford VIN

6R09K000001
6 — Last digit of model year
R — Assembly plant (R-San Jose)
09 — Body code (09 - Mustang 2dr 2+2)
K — Engine code, (271 hp 289 ci)
000001 — Consecutive unit number

### Location

Underneath Shelby VIN plate; stamped on driver's and passenger's side inner fender panel, near shock tower at outside edge; can only be seen with fender removed; stamped on engine block, beneath front exhaust port on passenger side.

## Carburetors

Holley R-3259
Ford C30F-9510-AB, AJ, C40F-9510-AD, AL, AT, or C4ZF-9510-G

## Distributors

C5GF-12127-A, C50F-12127-E, C5AZ-12127-EEZ

## 1966 Shelby Prices

| | Retail |
|---|---|
| Shelby GT350 | $4,428.00 |
| High performance Ford automatic transmission | N/C |
| Fold-down rear seat | 50.00 |
| AM radio | 57.50 |
| Alloy wheels | 268.00* |
| Stripe | 62.50 |
| Detroit No-Spin rear axle unit | 141.00 |
| Cobra Supercharger (Paxton) | 670.00 |

*Approximate price

## 1966 Shelby Exterior Colors

Wimbledon White
Candyapple Red
Sapphire Blue
Ivy Green
Raven Black

## 1966 Shelby Interior Trim

Black

## 1966 Shelby GT350 Facts

Visually, functional rear quarter panel scoops were added. The stock Mustang air extractor louvers were replaced with windows. All white GT350s came with blue rocker panel stripes. Other colors came with white rocker panel stripes. GT350H cars came with gold stripes with the exception of some early white Hertz cars which got blue stripes.

Some cars came with all steel hoods replacing the fiberglass/steel support hoods. A GT350 gas cap replaced the stock Mustang cap.

As with the 1965s, most of the Le Mans stripes were dealer installed, matching the rocker panel stripes in color.

In the interior, because the standard Mustang five-dial gauge panel was used, the center dash pod was eliminated. In its place stood a 9000 rpm Cobra tachometer. The Mustang rear seat replaced the fiberglass shelf, and with the exception of just 82 cars, all 1966 GT350s had the fold-down rear seats. The standard steering wheel was the Mustang optional Deluxe wheel with a GT350 logo.

Only the first 252 1966 cars had the lowered "A" arms because these were actually leftover 1965s updated for 1966. As a cost-cutting measure, subsequent cars used the standard mounting points. For the same reasons, the override traction bars were replaced on cars numbering 800 and above with bars that mounted beneath the axle, but as with most Shelbys, there were exceptions.

The rear exiting exhaust system replaced the side pipes of 1965.

GT350s with the three-speed automatic transmission came with a Ford 600 cfm carburetor replacing the Holley 715.

Relegated to the option list, factory or dealer, were Koni shocks, the Detroit Locker differential, and the wood-rimmed steering wheel.

Wheel selection was greater for 1966. The leftover cars came with either the silver-painted steel wheels or the Cragar mags, which could also be had on later cars. The standard wheel on later cars was a silver-painted 14 inch Magnum 500, but the Hertz cars came with chrome versions. The 14 inch Shelby aluminum ten-spoke wheels became optional on later cars. Some cars also came with plain 14 inch silver-painted wheels.

Early cars generally came with hollow-letter Cobra valve covers while later cars had solid letters and black crinkle finish.

One thousand GT350s were sold to Hertz and designated GT350H. Most were painted black and most had gold stripes. Some were equipped with the four-speed manual but the great majority came with the automatic transmission. Chrome Magnum 500 wheels were standard on these cars.

In April 1966, the Paxton Supercharger was made available as an option.

Six Shelby convertibles were built but not available for sale to the public. All had the automatic transmission and air conditioning. The side scoops were not functional as they would have interfered with the convertible top mechanism. Twelve continuation convertibles were built during 1980–82 to cash in on the Shelby phenomenon. The Shelby organization was still a functioning entity so these cars, built on refurbished original "K" convertibles, got the same Shelby identification as the original six.

*1966 Shelby GT350H*

# Chapter 29

# 1967 Shelby Mustang

## Production Figures

| | | | |
|---|---|---|---|
| GT350 | 1,175 | GT500 Convertible | |
| GT500 | 2,048 | prototype | 1 |
| GT500 Notchback | | Total | 3,225 |
| prototype | 1 | | |

## Shelby VIN
67200F2A00000

67 — Year

2 — Engine (2-289, 4-428)

0 — Transmission (0-4-speed, 1-automatic)

0 — Base vehicle component (0-base vehicle, 1-Ford air conditioning, 2-Thermactor exhaust emission, 3-air conditioning and Thermactor exhaust)

F — Body style (F-fastback)

2 — Exterior color code

A — Interior trim

00000 — Consecutive unit number, 00001 to 3225.

**Location**

Stamped plate is pop-riveted on driver's side inner front fender panel, over the Ford VIN; VIN is also stamped on passenger's side inner fender panel, halfway between the firewall and radiator.

## Ford VIN
7R02K00001

7 — Last digit of model year

R— Assembly plant (R-San Jose)

02 — Body code (02-2dr fastback)

K — Engine code (K-271 hp 289, Q-428 ci)

00001 — Consecutive unit number

**Location**

Stamped on driver's side fender panel, underneath the Shelby VIN plate; stamped on passenger's and driver's side inner front fender panel near the outside edge of the shock tower, visible only when fender is removed; on some GT350s, it is stamped on the engine block beneath the front exhaust port on passenger's side; on four-speed cars, it is stamped on the transmission case.

## GT350 Carburetor
Holley R-3259

## GT500 Carburetors
Front — Holley R-2804

Rear — Holley R-2805

## GT350 Distributors
C5GF-12127-A, C50F-12127-E, C5AZ-12127-EEZ

## GT500 Distributor
C5AF-12127-E

## 1967 Shelby Prices

| | Retail |
|---|---|
| GT350 | $3,995.00 |
| GT500 | 4,195.00 |
| Power disc brakes | 64.77 |
| Power steering | 84.47 |
| Shoulder harness | 50.76 |
| Select-O-Matic transmission | 50.00 |
| Air conditioner, SelectAire | 356.09 |
| Exhaust emission control system | 45.45 |
| Closed crankcase emission system | 5.19 |
| Fold-down rear seat | 64.77 |
| Radio, AM push-button | 57.51 |
| Deluxe wheels | 185.00 |
| Rallye stripe | 34.95 |
| Paxton Supercharger (GT350 only) | 549.00 |

## 1967 Shelby Exterior Colors

| | Code |
|---|---|
| Bronze Metallic | 1 |
| Dark Blue Metallic | 2 |
| Raven Black | 3 |
| Wimbledon White | 4 |
| Dark Moss Green | 5 |
| Medium Metallic Gray | 6 |
| Lime Green | 7 |
| Brittany Blue | 8 |
| Red | 0 |
| Medium Blue/ | |

## 1967 Shelby Exterior Colors

| | Code |
|---|---|
| Acapulco Blue | |
| Silver Frost | |

## 1967 Shelby Interior Trim

| | Code |
|---|---|
| Black | A |
| Parchment or white | U |

Some early cars have no interior code on the VIN.

## 1967 Shelby Facts

Two Shelby Mustangs were available in 1967, the GT350 sporting the high performance 289 V-8 and the GT500 with its larger 428 ci V-8.

While the 1965-66 bore great resemblance to the production Mustang, the 1967 Shelby was drastically restyled to emphasize the look of performance, as well as delivering performance. A fiberglass nose extension, which exaggerated the production Mustang look, housed a unique grille with two 7 inch driving lights. Most 1967 Shelbys have these lights mounted close to each other in the center of the grille; others have them mounted at each end of the grille opening to comply with certain states lighting laws. As the nose was extended by three inches, a unique fiberglass hood with a functional scoop was used. Additional hood pins were used to secure the hood. Upper and lower scoops were used in the rear; the lower scoops were functional on early cars but non-functional on the rest. At the rear, a fiberglass deck lid with a pronounced spoiler was used. Taillights were from the 1967 Cougar but without the chrome trim.

The Deluxe Mustang interior in either black or parchment (or white) was dominated by a two-point roll bar (some early cars had a four-point) which was the anchoring point for a pair of inertia-reel harnesses. The fold-down seat was a mandatory option, and all cars had a 140 mph speedometer and 8000 rpm tachometer. Additional Stewart Warner gauges, oil pressure and amps, were mounted in a special housing underneath the dash.

All 1967 Shelby Mustangs came with the familiar GT350 or GT500 rocker panel stripes, a front grille emblem, front fender emblems, rear deck emblem and a pop-open gas cap that had a Shelby Cobra cover. Some early cars have flat gas caps; most others have curved caps.

The GT350 came with the modified 271 hp 289 ci which was again rated at 306 hp. These did not have the steel Tri-Y headers and most did not have the Cobra oil pan. Four-speed models used a Holley 715 cfm carburetor while automatics got a Ford 595 cfm four-barrel. Most early GT350s used the S2MS numbered aluminum high-rise intake manifolds while later cars used the S7MS unit. In all other respects, the 289 was the same as the 1966 model. The GT500 came with a modified version of Ford's 428 ci Police Interceptor V-8. It used a pair of rear-mounted 600 cfm Holley carburetors on an aluminum intake manifold. An oval Cobra finned air cleaner matched the Cobra Lemans aluminum finned valve covers. The 428 was rated at 355 hp.

A very small number of the more powerful (425 hp) 427 Medium Riser V-8s were installed at the factory or at the selling dealer; the exact number is unknown. Extensive substantiation is required for the would-be purchaser.

The Paxton Supercharger was still available as an option on the GT350.

The standard Shelby wheel was a steel rim with a wheel cover. These are quite rare. More common are the Kelsey-Hayes styled steel wheels or the cast aluminum Shelby ten-spoke wheels, which measure 15x7 inches.

Some 1967 cars have 3 inch round tailpipe extensions; others used the quad exhaust extensions from the Mustang GT.

Some Shelby VIN tags were hand-lettered; most cars with the outboard headlights also have the letter "Z" preceding the serial number on the VIN plate.

*1967 Shelby GT500*

# Chapter 30

# 1968 Shelby Mustang

## Production Figures

| | | | |
|---|---|---|---|
| GT350 Fastback | 1,253 | GT500KR Fastback | 933 |
| GT350 Convertible | 404 | GT500KR Convertible | 318 |
| GT500 Fastback | 1,140 | Total | 4,450 |
| GT500 Convertible | 402 | | |

## Shelby VIN

8T02J000001-00001

8 — Last digit of model year
T — Assembly plant (T-Metuchen)
02 — Body code (02-fastback, 03-convertible)
J — Engine code (J-302, S-428, R-428CJ-R)
000001 — Consecutive unit number
00001 — Consecutive Shelby production number, 00001 to 04450.

### Location

Stamped on plate which is pop-riveted on driver's side inner front fender panel over Ford VIN.

## Ford VIN

Exactly the same as the Shelby VIN but without the consecutive Shelby production number.

### Location

Stamped on driver's side inner fender panel, underneath Shelby VIN plate; stamped on plate riveted on instrument panel on passenger side, visible through windshield; stamped on warranty plate on driver's door rear face, which also reads "Special Performance Vehicle."

## Distributors

GT350 — C8ZF-12127-A/manual, C8ZF-12127-D/automatic
GT500 — C8AF-12127-J
GT500KR — C8AF-12127-T

## Carburetors

GT350 — Holley R-4069
GT500 — Holley R-4129
GT500KR — Holley R-4168/manual, Holley R-4174/automatic

## 1968 Shelby Prices

| | Retail |
|---|---|
| GT350 Fastback | $4,116.62 |
| GT350 Convertible | 4,238.14 |
| GT500 Fastback | 4,317.39 |
| GT500 Convertible | 4,438.91 |

| | |
|---|---|
| GT500KR Fastback | 4,472.57 |
| GT500KR Convertible | 4,594.09 |
| Power disc brakes | 64.77 |
| Power steering | 84.47 |
| Shoulder harness | 50.76 |
| Fold-down rear seat (Fastbacks only) | 64.78 |
| Radio, AM push-button | 57.59 |
| Select-O-Matic transmission | 50.08 |
| Tinted glass (air conditioned cars only—required) | 30.25 |
| Tilt-away steering wheel | 62.18 |

## 1968 Shelby Exterior Colors

| | Code |
|---|---|
| Raven Black | A |
| Lime Green Metallic | I |
| Wimbledon White | M |
| Medium Blue Metallic | Q |
| Dark Green Metallic | R |
| Candyapple Red | T |
| Meadowlark Yellow | W |
| Dark Blue Metallic | X |
| Gold Metallic | Y |
| Orange | |

## 1968 Shelby Interior Trim

| | Code |
|---|---|
| Black | 6A |
| Saddle | 6F |

## Convertible Top Colors

Black
White

## 1968 Shelby Facts

Production of the Shelby continued, but under Ford control and at the A.O. Smith Company facility in Livonia, Michigan. A new body style joined the line-up—the convertible available in either a GT350 or GT500. Officially, the 1968 cars were renamed Shelby Mustang Cobra GT350/GT500/GT500KR, reflecting Ford's proclivity to use the Cobra name in all its performance applications.

Although there wasn't much of a difference mechanically between a 1967 and a 1968 Shelby, the 1968 nose was restyled. The new look was decidedly Mustang, yet with a much more aggressive look. Fiberglass was again used to create the new front end treatment. The grille opening housed either Lucas or Marchal foglamps while the hood used twin front hood scoops with a set of rear hood louvers.

New Cobra emblems were used on the front fenders and on the passenger side of the dash panel. The interior was Deluxe Mustang in either black or saddle but the Shelby used a console which housed two Stewart Warner gauges—oil pressure and amps. The console storage compartment had a Cobra embossed top. The roll bars with the inertia-reel harnesses were used on all Shelbys with the exception of the convertible, which used a unique padded bar.

Standard wheels were steel with a mag style wheel cover. Optional were the ten-spoke Shelby wheels. These wheels were cast differently than the 1967 versions and will have ball joint interference if installed on a 1967 Shelby.

The GT350 lost some of its zip as the High Performance 289 was replaced by a production 302 V-8. The 302 did use an aluminum Cobra intake manifold and Holley 600 cfm carburetor for a 250 hp rating. The 302 used a Cobra oval air cleaner and Cobra valve covers. Functional Ram Air was optional. The Paxton Supercharger was optional on the GT350; additional gauges—fuel pressure and boost—were mounted on the console.

The GT500 again got the 428 ci Police Interceptor V-8 rated at 360 hp even though it came with only a single 715 cfm Holley carburetor mounted on an aluminum manifold. A few GT500s have the 427 Low Riser engine which was available only with an automatic transmission. The letter "W" must be present in the VIN for an original factory installed 427.

The GT500KR replaced the GT500 when the 428 Cobra Jet engine became available. Underrated at 335 hp, it put out close to 400 hp and the GT500KR had the same features found on the 1968½ Cobra Jet Mustang. KRs got Cobra Jet emblems on the fenders, dash and gas cap lid. All KRs had functional Ram Air which meant no Cobra oval aircleaner.

*1968 Shelby GT500 convertible*

*1968 Shelby GT500KR Fastback*

# Chapter 31

# 1969-70 Shelby Mustang

## Production Figures*

| | |
|---|---|
| Barrier Test & Prototype Pilot cars | 3 |
| GT350 Fastbacks | 935 |
| GT500 Fastback Hertz cars | 150 |
| GT350 Convertibles | 194 |
| GT500 Fastback | 1,536 |
| GT500 Convertibles | 335 |
| Total — 1969 | 3,153** |
| 1970 models | 789 |
| Grand Total, 1969 and 1970 | 3,942 |

*SAAC considers these figures approximate, based on FOMOCO document dated 12/23/69.

**1969 total based on highest serial number located is 3294. Until 1969, consecutive unit numbers matched with the number of cars built. In 1969, however, highest serial number located is 3294, but according to other sources, production that is accounted for totals 3153—thus the uncertainty.

## Serial Numbers

9F02M480001

9 — Last digit of model year (0-1970 updated cars)
F — Assembly plant (F-Dearborn)
M — Engine code (M-351, R-428CJ-R)
48 — Shelby code
0001 — Consecutive unit number

### Location

Plate riveted to dash panel on driver's side, visible through windshield; stamped on warranty plate located on face of driver's door, which also reads "Special Performance Vehicle"; stamped on driver's and passenger's inner fender panel halfway between shock tower and firewall, visible with fenders removed; additional plate stating "Custom-Crafted by Shelby Automotive, Inc." attached above warranty plate.

## Distributors

GT350- C90F-12127-M or N/manual, C90F-12127-M or T/automatic
GT500- C8AF-12127-T

## Carburetors

GT350- C9ZF-9510-C/manual, C9ZF-9510-D/automatic
GT500- Holley R-4279/manual, R-4280/automatic

## 1969 Shelby Prices

| | Retail |
|---|---|
| GT350 SportsRoof | $4,434.00 |
| GT350 Convertible | 4,753.00 |
| GT500 SportsRoof | 4,709.00 |
| GT500 Convertible | 5,027.00 |

| | |
|---|---:|
| Close ratio 4–speed transmission (GT350 only, std. GT500) | N/C |
| Automatic transmission | 30.54 |
| Air conditioning | 374.39 |
| Optional axle ratio | 6.13 |
| Traction-Lok differential | 60.97 |
| Drag Package | 155.45 |
| Sport Deck rear seat (fastback only) | 91.51 |
| Tilt-away steering wheel | 62.24 |
| Power ventilation | 37.83 |
| AM radio | 57.38 |
| AM/FM stereo | 170.76 |
| Stereo tape (requires AM radio) | 125.64 |
| Intermittent windshield wipers | 15.85 |
| Tinted glass | 30.54 |
| Heavy-duty batteries (GT350 only) | |
| Option #1 | 7.93 |
| Option #2 | 15.85 |
| F60x15 Goodyear tires, extra heavy-duty Suspension Package | 60.97 |

## 1969–70 Shelby Exterior Colors

| | Code |
|---|---|
| Acapulco Blue | D |
| Black Jade | C |
| Silver Jade | 4 |
| Gulfstream Aqua | F |
| Pastel Gray | 6 |
| Candyapple Red | T |
| Royal Maroon | B |
| Grabber Blue | J |
| Grabber Green | Z |
| Grabber Yellow | |
| Grabber Orange | U |

## 1969–70 Shelby Interior Trim

| | Code |
|---|---|
| Black | 3A |
| White | 3W |
| Red | 3D |

## Convertible Top Colors

Black
White

## 1969–70 Shelby Facts

This was the last year for the Shelby Mustangs. Based on the new SportsRoof and convertible Mustang body styles, the Shelby's styling was unique and bore little resemblance to the production Mustang. Two models were available, the GT350 and GT500, each in a fastback or convertible.

The front end styling was a complete departure from previous Shelby Mustangs. Fiberglass fenders and hood created a large rectangular grille opening which houses two 7 inch headlights. Lucas foglamps were mounted beneath the bumper. The hood had three forward-facing NASA scoops (the center one providing air to the engine's intake system) and two rear-facing scoops. The front fenders also had brake scoops, as did the rear, which provided air to the brakes. The convertibles used a rear scoop that was mounted lower to prevent interference with the convertible top mechanism. The rear of the car used a fiberglass deck lid and extensions to form a pronounced spoiler. 1965 Thunderbird lights were utilized, and the Shelby used a unique aluminum exhaust collector exiting in the center beneath the bumper.

Side stripes ran the length of the car's sides with either GT350 or GT500 lettering at the front fender in front of the brake scoop. Snake emblems were located behind the rear side windows and on the left side of the front grille. Cobra Jet emblems, like the ones on the 1968 GT500KR, were used on the GT500's front fenders.

The interior was the Mustang's Deluxe Interior Decor Group, in black or white, with Shelby identification on the door panels, steering wheel and passenger's dash. The console top had two Stewart Warner gauges, oil pressure and amps, and two toggle switches for the foglamps and courtesy lights. The instrument cluster contained temperature, 8000 rpm tachometer, 140 mph speedometer and fuel gauges. All fastback Shelbys have roll bars with the inertia-reel harnesses while the convertibles used the same 1968 type roll bar. A small number of Shelby Mustangs came with red interiors.

The GT350 came with the 290 hp four-barrel version of the 351 Windsor engine. The only difference between it and other 351s was the use of an aluminum intake manifold and Cobra valve covers.

The GT500 used the 428CJ-R V-8 with all the regular Mustang variations applying to the Shelby (see 1969 Mustang).

The Competition Suspension, transmission and rear axle options paralleled those found on the Mach 1.

Wheels were unique to the Shelby. The 15x7 inch rims used an aluminum center section welded to a chrome steel rim. Standard tires were E70x15; most cars came with F60x15 Goodyear Polyglas GTs.

Other standard features included power steering, power front disc brakes, and four-speed manual transmission.

About 789 cars were unsold in 1969. These were "updated" and sold as 1970 models by changing the VIN to reflect 1970 as the model year. Other changes were the twin black hood stripes and a Boss 302 type chin spoiler.

*1969 Shelby GT500 convertible*

*1969 Shelby GT500 SportsRoof*

*1970 Shelby GT350 convertible*

# Appendix

## Warranty Plates and Certification Labels

Three different Warranty Plates were used on 1965-69 Mustangs; however, they all displayed the same information. The warranty number was the same as the Mustang's VIN, while the rest of the codes indicated body style, color code, trim code, date built code, District Sales Office (DSO), axle and transmission codes. If the color code was missing, that meant that this Mustang came with a Special Order non-stock color.

From 1970-78, a label replaced the metal plate with the only major difference being the month and year were shown rather than date and month for the build date.

During 1979-80, the label was again revised to include additional information such as air conditioning code, vinyl roof color code and weight. In addition to month and year, scheduled date was included showing date and month of assembly.

The label was again changed slightly from 1981-90 to include suspension, sunroof/moonroof, and bodyside molding codes.

## Casting Dates and Manufacturing Dates

All Mustang parts have date codes that are either cast or stamped or both on that part. Date codes that are cast into the part indicate the date the part was cast. Manufacture dates are stamped into the part. These date codes are fairly simple to decipher. For example, if a part has the date 9 B 16, it can be understood as follows:

9 — year, in this case, 1969

B — month, February

16 — day of month

Parts installed into a Mustang were cast or manufactured before the car was actually built. This means that date codes could be as much as thirty days before actual vehicle manufacture. This may be important in ascertaining a Mustang's originality.

## Sheet Metal Date Codes

In much the same way, Mustang sheet metal was stamped to show the date it was manufactured. For example, a sheet metal part with 10 5 D 1 breaks down as follows:

10 — Month(October)

5 — Date

D — Stamping plant(Dearborn)

1 — Shift (first shift)

Although sheet metal date codes do not indicate year of manufacture, as with other components, the stamping date will fall before vehicle manufacture, up to 30 days.

| BODY | COLOR | TRIM | DATE | DSO | AXLE | TRANS |
|------|-------|------|------|-----|------|-------|
| 65A | J | 25 | 3H | 33 | 1 | 6 |

VEHICLE WARRANTY NUMBER

5S07C250001

*Ford*

NOT FOR TITLE OR
REGISTRATION PURPOSES

THIS VEHICLE IS MANUFACTURED UNDER UNITED STATES
AND FOREIGN PATENTS AND PATENT APPLICATIONS

A PRODUCT OF *Ford* MOTOR COMPANY

*1965*

| 6F07C100001 | | | WARRANTY NUMBER | *Ford* | MADE IN U.S.A. |
|-------------|---|---|----------------|--------|----------------|

NOT FOR TITLE OR REGISTRATION

| 65A | M | 25 | 3H | 33 | 1 | 6 |
|------|-------|------|------|-----|------|-------|
| BODY | COLOR | TRIM | DATE | DSO | AXLE | TRANS |

*Ford*

*1966–68*

NOT FOR TITLE OR REGISTRATION

9T02Q100001   WARRANTY NUMBER *Ford*   MADE IN U.S.A.

*Ford*

| 63C | A | 3D | 27J | 61 | V | 5 |
|------|-------|------|------|-----|------|-------|
| BODY | COLOR | TRIM | DATE | DSO | AXLE | TRANS |

*1969*

MANUFACTURED BY                  100001
FORD MOTOR COMPANY

08/70 THIS VEHICLE CONFORMS
TO ALL APPLICABLE FEDERAL
MOTOR VEHICLE SAFETY STAN-
DARDS IN EFFECT ON DATE OF
MANUFACTURE SHOWN ABOVE

| VEH. IDENT NO. | BODY | COL. |
|----------------|------|------|
| 1F01M100001 | 65D | P |

| TRIM | AXLE | TRNS. | DSO |
|------|------|-------|-----|
| 1R | 6 | U | 11 |

NOT FOR TITLE OR REGISTRATION

MADE IN U.S.A.

*1970–78*

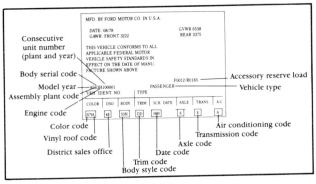

*1979–80*

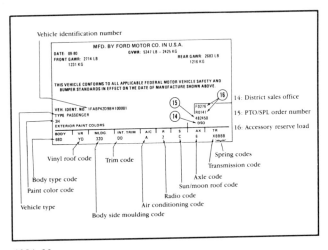

*1981–90*

Third generation Mustang sheet metal is dated the same way. However, replacement sheet metal will also have a month and year code, such as 9 85 (September 1985), preceding the regular date code.

## District Codes (DSOs)

Units built on a Domestic Special Order, Foreign Special Order or other special orders will have the complete order number in this space. Also to appear in this space is the two-digit code number of the district which ordered the unit. If the unit is a regular production unit, only the district code number will appear.

That is the typical DSO explanation found in Ford shop manuals. A DSO is an internal Ford production code which groups batches of similarly equipped cars to be built at the same time so that the specific parts used would be correctly scheduled to be on the assembly line as this group of cars was rolling down the line. Thus a group of Mustang LXs destined for the California Highway Patrol would get a specific DSO number plus the two-digit code for L.A. (for example) which is 71.

| Code | District | Code | District | Code | District |
|------|----------|------|----------|------|----------|
| 11 | Boston | 41 | Chicago | 71 | Los Angeles |
| 13 | New York | 43 | Milwaukee | 72 | San Jose |
| 15 | Newark | 44 | Twin Cities | 73 | Salt Lake City |
| 16 | Philadelphia | 45 | Davenport | 74 | Seattle |
| 17 | Washington | 46 | Indianapolis | 75 | Phoenix |
| 21 | Atlanta | 47 | Cincinnati | 81 | Ford of |
| 22 | Charlotte | 51 | Denver | | Canada |
| 24 | Jacksonville | 52 | Des Moines | 83 | Government |
| 25 | Richmond | 53 | Kansas City | 84 | Home Office |
| 27 | Cincinnati | 54 | Omaha | | Reserve |
| 28 | Louisville | 55 | St. Louis | 85 | American |
| 32 | Cleveland | 56 | Davenport | | Red Cross |
| 33 | Detroit | 61 | Dallas | 87 | Body |
| 34 | Indianapolis | 62 | Houston | | Company |
| 35 | Lansing | 63 | Memphis | 89 | Transport |
| 37 | Buffalo | 64 | New Orleans | | Services |
| 38 | Pittsburgh | 65 | Oklahoma City | 90–99 | Export |

## Date Codes

| Month | Code first year | Code second year (if model year exceeds twelve months) |
|-------|-----------------|---------------------------------------------------------|
| January | A | N |
| February | B | P |
| March | C | Q |
| April | D | R |
| May | E | S |
| June | F | T |
| July | G | U |
| August | H | V |
| September | J | W |
| October | K | X |
| November | L | Y |
| December | M | Z |

## Mustang transmissions 1965–73

| | Code |
|---|------|
| Three-speed manual | 1 |
| Four-speed manual, wide ratio | 5 |

## Mustang transmissions 1965–73

| | Code |
|---|------|
| Four-speed manual, close ratio | 6 (1967–71) |
| Four-speed manual, close ratio | E (1972–73) |

141

## Mustang transmissions 1965-73

|  | Code |
|---|---|
| Three-speed automatic *C4* | W |
| Three-speed automatic *FMX* | X |
| Three-speed automatic *C6* | U |

## Mustang transmissions 1974-90

|  | Code |
|---|---|
| Four-speed overdrive (SROD) | 4 |
| Five-speed manual | 5 |
| Five-speed manual overdrive (RAP) | 5 |

## Mustang transmissions 1974-90

|  | Code |
|---|---|
| Four-speed manual (Borg-Warner) | 6 |
| Four-speed overdrive (RUG) | 7 |
| Four-speed (ET) | 7 |
| Three-speed automatic *C3* | V |
| Three-speed automatic *C4* | W |
| Three-speed automatic *C5* | C |
| AOD (automatic overdrive) | T |
| C-6 Police automatic | Z |

## Mustang specifications

|  | 1965-66 | 1967-68 | 1969-70 | 1971-73 | 1974-78 | 1979-90 |
|---|---|---|---|---|---|---|
| Wheelbase, in. | 108 | 108 | 108 | 109 | 96.2 | 100.4 |
| Track, frt./ rear, in. | 56/56 | 58.1/58/1 | 58.5/58.5 | 61.5/61.5 | 55.6/55.8 | 56.6/57 |
| Width, in. | 68.2 | 70.9 | 71.8 | 74.1 | 70.2 | 69.1 |
| Height in. | 51 | 51.8 | 50.3 | 50.1 | 50.3 | 51.9 |
| Length in. | 181.6 | 183.6 | 187.4 | 189.5[1] | 175 | 179.1 |
| Curb weight, lb. | 2,860 (289) | 2,980 (302) | 3,625 (428CJ) | 3,560 (351CJ) | 3,290 (302) | 2,861 (140)[2] |
| Wt. dist., % f/r | 53/47 (289) | 56/44 (302) | 59/41 (428CJ) | 56.5/43.5 (351) | 59/41 | 57/43[3] |

*1—193.8 in 1973       2—3075 with 302          3—59/41 with 302*

Rear axle codes — 1965–1990

| Axle | 1965 | 1966 | 1967 | 1968 | 1969 | 1970 | 1971 | 1972 | 1973 | 1974 | 1975-76 |
|---|---|---|---|---|---|---|---|---|---|---|---|
| 2.35 |  |  |  |  | F |  |  |  |  |  |  |
| 2.47 |  |  |  |  |  |  |  |  |  |  |  |
| 2.50 |  |  |  |  |  |  |  |  |  |  |  |
| 2.73 |  |  |  | O |  |  |  |  |  |  |  |
| 2.75 |  |  | 8(H) |  | 2(K) | 2(K) | 2(K) | 2(K) | 2(K) |  |  |
| 2.79 |  |  |  |  | 3 | 3 | 3 | 3 | 3 |  |  |
| 2.80 | 6(F) | 6(F) | 6(F) | 1(A) | 4(M) | 4(M) | 4(M) |  |  |  |  |
| 2.83 | 2(B) | 2(B) | 2(B) | 2(B) | 5 | 5 |  |  |  |  |  |
| 3.00 | 1(A) | 1(A) | 1(A) | 3(C) | 6(O) | 6 | 6 | 6 | 6(O) |  | 6(O) |
| 3.07 |  |  |  | 4(D) |  | B | B |  |  |  |  |
| 3.08 |  |  |  | 5(E) | C(U) | C |  |  |  |  |  |
| 3.10 |  |  |  |  | 7 |  |  |  |  |  |  |
| 3.18 |  |  |  |  |  |  |  |  |  |  |  |
| 3.20 | 3(C) | 3(C) | 3(C) | 6(F) |  | 8 |  |  |  |  |  |
| 3.25 | 4(D) | 4(D) | 4(D) | 7(G) | 9(R) | 9(R) |  | 9(R) |  |  |  |
| 3.27 |  |  |  |  |  |  |  |  |  |  | 7 |
| 3.40 |  |  |  |  |  |  |  |  |  |  |  |
| 3.45 |  |  |  |  |  |  |  |  |  |  |  |
| 3.50 | 5(E) | 5(E) | 5(E) | 8(H) | A(S) | A(S) | 9(R) | A(S) | 9(R) |  |  |
| 3.55 |  |  |  |  |  |  |  |  |  | G(X) | G(X) |
| 3.73 |  | 8(H) |  |  |  |  | A(S) |  | A(S) |  |  |
| 3.89 | 8(H) |  |  |  |  |  |  |  |  |  |  |
| 3.91 |  |  |  |  | (V) | (V) | (V) | (V) |  |  |  |
| 4.11 | 9(I) | 9(I) | 9(I) |  |  |  | (Y) |  |  |  |  |
| 4.30 |  |  |  |  | (W) | (W) | (Y) |  |  |  |  |

*Letter in parentheses indicates locking differential.*

143

**Rear axle codes — 1965-1990**

| Axle | 1977-78 | 1979 | 1980 | 1981 | 1982 | 1983 | 1984 | 1985 | 1986 | 1987 | 1988 | 1989 | 1990 |
|---|---|---|---|---|---|---|---|---|---|---|---|---|---|
| 2.35 | | | | | | | | | | | | | |
| 2.47 | | B | B(C) | B(C) | B(C) | | | | | | | | |
| 2.50 | | | | | | | | | | | | | |
| 2.73 | | | 8 | 8(M) | 8(M) | 8(M) | 8(M) | 8(M) | 8(M) | 8(M) | 8(M) | 8(M) | 8(M) |
| 2.75 | 3 | | | | | | | | | | | | |
| 2.79 | | | | | | | | | | | | | |
| 2.80 | | | | | | | | | | | | | |
| 2.83 | | | | | | | | | | | | | |
| 3.00 | | | | | | | | | | | | | |
| 3.07 | | | | | | | | | | | | | |
| 3.08 | | Y(Z) | Y(Z) | Y(Z) | Y(Z) | Y(Z) | Y(Z) | Y(Z) | Y(Z) | Y(Z) | Y(Z) | Y(Z) | Y(Z) |
| 3.10 | 4 | | | | | | | | | | | | |
| 3.18 | | | | | | | | | | | | | |
| 3.20 | | | | | | | | | | | | | |
| 3.25 | | | | | | | | | | | | | |
| 3.27 | | | | | | 5(E) | 5(E) | 5(E) | 5(E) | 5(E) | 5(E) | 5(E) | 5(E) |
| 3.40 | | | | | | | | | | | | | |
| 3.45 | | F(R) | F(R) | F(R) | F(R) | F(R) | F(R) | F(R) | F(R) | F(R) | F(R) | F(R) | F(R) |
| 3.50 | | | | | | | | | | | | | |
| 3.55 | | | | | | | | (W) | (W) | | | | |
| 3.73 | | | | | | | | | | | | | |
| 3.89 | | | | | | | | | | | | | |
| 3.91 | | | | | | | | | | | | | |
| 4.11 | | | | | | | | | | | | | |
| 4.30 | | | | | | | | | | | | | |

*Letter in parentheses indicates locking differential.*